HANK AARON

HANK AARON

A BIOGRAPHY

CHARLIE VASCELLARO

BASEBALL'S ALL-TIME GREATEST HITTERS

GREENWOOD PRESS

WESTPORT, CONNECTICUT • LONDON

Library of Congress Cataloging-in-Publication Data

Vascellaro, Charlie.
　　Hank Aaron : a biography / Charlie Vascellaro.
　　　　p.　cm.—(Baseball's all-time greatest hitters)
　　Includes bibliographical references and index.
　　ISBN 0–313–33001–8 (alk. paper)
　　1. Baseball players—United States—Biography.　I. Title.　II. Series.
GV865.A25V37　2005
796.357'092—dc22　　　　2004023601

British Library Cataloguing in Publication Data is available.

Library of Congress Catalog Card Number: 2004023601
ISBN: 0–313–33001–8

First published in 2005

Greenwood Press, 88 Post Road West, Westport, CT 06881
An imprint of Greenwood Publishing Group, Inc.
www.greenwood.com

Printed in the United States of America

The paper used in this book complies with the
Permanent Paper Standard issued by the National
Information Standards Organization (Z39.48–1984).

10 9 8 7 6 5 4 3 2 1

Every reasonable effort has been made to trace the owners of copyright
materials in this book, but in some instances this has proven impossible.
The author and publisher will be glad to receive information leading to
more complete acknowledgments in subsequent printings of the book
and in the meantime extend their apologies for any omissions.

For my teachers: Mark Harris (Creative Writing) and Cordelia Candelaria (Baseball Fiction) at Arizona State University, Jim Martin (Journalism) at Scottsdale Community College, the former Ms. Marcia Tower (English) from Coronado High School, and sixth-grade teacher Mr. Zurowski, (everything and baseball too) at North Country Elementary. All of you continue to be sources of inspiration.

I, Too, Sing America
I, too, sing America.

I am the darker brother.
They send me to eat in the kitchen
When company comes,
But I laugh,
And eat well,
And grow strong.

Tomorrow,
I'll be at the table
When company comes.
Nobody'll dare
Say to me,
"Eat in the kitchen,"
Then.

Besides,
They'll see how beautiful I am
And be ashamed—

I, too, am America.
                                   —Langston Hughes

CONTENTS

Contents

SERIES FOREWORD

The volumes in Greenwood's "Baseball's All-Time Greatest Hitters" series present the life stories of the players who, through their abilities to hit for average, for power, or for both, most helped their teams at the plate. Much thought was given to the players selected for inclusion in this series. In some cases, the selection of certain players was a given. **Ty Cobb**, **Rogers Hornsby**, and **Joe Jackson** hold the three highest career averages in baseball history: .367, .358, and .356, respectively. **Babe Ruth**, who single-handedly brought the sport out of its "dead ball" era and transformed baseball into a home-run hitters game, hit 714 home runs (a record that stood until 1974) while also hitting .342 over his career. **Lou Gehrig**, now known primarily as the man whose consecutive-games record Cal Ripken Jr. broke in 1995, hit .340 and knocked in more than 100 runs eleven seasons in a row, totaling 1,995 before his career was cut short by ALS. **Ted Williams**, the last man in either league to hit .400 or better in a season (.406 in 1941), is widely regarded as possibly the best hitter ever, a man whose fanatical dedication raised hitting to the level of both science and art.

Two players set career records that, for many, define the art of hitting. **Hank Aaron** set career records for home runs (755) and RBIs (2,297). He also maintained a .305 career average over twenty-three seasons, a remarkable feat for someone primarily known as a home-run hitter. **Pete Rose** had ten seasons with 200 or more hits and won three batting titles on his way to establishing his famous record of 4,256 career hits. Some critics have claimed that both players' records rest more on longevity than excellence. To that I would say there is something to be said about longevity and, in both cases, the player's excellence was the reason why he had the opportunity to keep playing, to keep tallying hits for his team. A base hit is the mark of a successful plate appearance; a home run is the apex of an at-bat. Accordingly, we could hardly have a series titled "Baseball's All-Time Greatest Hitters" without including the two men who set the career records in these categories.

Joe DiMaggio holds another famous mark: fifty-six consecutive games in which he obtained a base hit. Many have called this baseball's most unbreakable record. (The player who most closely approached that mark was Pete Rose, who hit safely in forty-four consecutive games in 1978.) In his thirteen seasons, DiMaggio hit .325 with 361 home runs and 1,537 RBIs. This means he *averaged* 28 home runs and 118 RBIs per season. MVPs have been awarded to sluggers in various years with lesser stats than what DiMaggio achieved in an "average" season.

Because **Stan Musial** played his entire career with the Cardinals in St. Louis—once considered the western frontier of the baseball world in the days before baseball came to California—he did not receive the press of a DiMaggio. But Musial compiled a career average of .331, with 3,630 hits (ranking fourth all time) and 1,951 RBIs (fifth all time). His hitting prowess was so respected around the league that Brooklyn Dodgers fans once dubbed him "The Man," a nickname he still carries today.

Willie Mays was a player who made his fame in New York City and then helped usher baseball into the modern era when he moved with the Giants to San Francisco. Mays did everything well and with flair. His over-the-shoulder catch in the 1954 World Series was perhaps his most famous moment, but his hitting was how Mays most tormented his opponents. Over twenty-two seasons the "Say Hey Kid" hit .302 and belted 660 home runs.

Only four players have reached the 600-home-run milestone: Mays, Aaron, Ruth, and **Barry Bonds**, who achieved that feat in 2002. Bonds, the only active player included in this series, broke the single-season home-run record when he smashed 73 for the San Francisco Giants in 2001. In the 2002 National League Championship Series, St. Louis Cardinals pitchers were so leery of pitching to him that they walked him ten times in twenty-one plate appearances. In the World Series, the Anaheim Angels walked him thirteen times in thirty appearances. He finished the Series with a .471 batting average, an on-base percentage of .700, and a slugging percentage of 1.294.

As with most rankings, this series omits some great names. Jimmie Foxx, Tris Speaker, and Tony Gwynn would have battled for a hypothetical thirteenth volume. And it should be noted that this series focuses on players and their performance within Major League Baseball; otherwise, sluggers such as Josh Gibson from the Negro Leagues and Japan's Sadaharu Oh would have merited consideration.

There are names such as Cap Anson, Ed Delahanty, and Billy Hamilton who appear high up on the list of career batting average. However, a number of these players played during the late 1800s, when the rules of baseball were drastically different. For example, pitchers were not allowed to throw overhand until 1883, and foul balls weren't counted as strikes until 1901 (1903 in the American League). Such players as Anson and company undeniably were the stars of their day, but baseball has evolved greatly since then, into a game in which hitters must now cope with night games, relief pitchers, and split-fingered fastballs.

Ultimately, a list of the "greatest" anything is somewhat subjective, but Greenwood offers these players as twelve of the finest examples of hitters throughout history. Each volume focuses primarily on the playing career of the subject: his early years in school, his years in semi-pro and/or minor league baseball, his entrance into the majors, and his ascension to the status of a legendary hitter. But even with the greatest of players, baseball is only part of the story, so the player's life before and after baseball is given significant consideration. And because no one can exist in a vacuum, the authors often take care to recreate the cultural and historical contexts of the time—an approach that is especially relevant to the multidisciplinary ways in which sports are studied today.

Batter up.

ROB KIRKPATRICK
GREENWOOD PUBLISHING

ACKNOWLEDGMENTS

Of great inspiration during the writing of this book and a lifetime spent as a reader of baseball history in previous decades were the biographies and autobiographies written about and with Henry (Hank) Aaron. While there may be factual discrepancies and at times contradictory viewpoints contained within the various accounts of his life, all are consistent in their inspirational tone, which is a testament to Aaron's legacy.

Beginning as a young reader picking up books for the first time, Aaron's life story served as an early introduction to serious reading and intellectual inquiry. Thirty years later, I can still recall watching Aaron's record-breaking, society-shaking 715th home run on television. At the same time, I remember the Scholastic Book Fairs periodically held in my elementary school cafeteria. Completely captivated by baseball in general and Hank Aaron in particular, I purchased books for 75 cents or $1.25 that transported me; they elevated my consciousness and conscience. Hank Aaron's story changed the way I viewed the world. I didn't have to be an African American to understand injustice. The story of his Aaron's life presented clear descriptions of right and wrong. In open defiance to hostile adversity, his story also proved and continues to prove that anything is possible. His dream come true is the American Dream fulfilled. If a poor, black child from rural Alabama, raised in a ramshackle shack without plumbing and electricity, could grow up to be the all-time home-run king, then anything is possible.

The bindings on these paperbacks are torn and frayed, they have scribbled pencil drawings on their blank pages, vocabulary words, new to me at the time, are underlined. I've carried these books with me from childhood homes to first apartments, from the East Coast to the West and back again. Almost twenty years after reading Joel H. Cohen's *Hammerin' Hank of the Atlanta Braves*, and Phil Musick's *Hank Aaron: The Man Who Beat the Babe*, Aaron's own 1991 autobiography *I Had a Hammer*, written with Lonnie Wheeler, would become the most inspirational book I've read. I carried it around with me while attending college. I read it in my lap during class, sneaking peeks at pages whenever I could get a chance. (Aaron signed it for me in the press box at Scottsdale Stadium, even though it was against the rules. "No Autographs" was written clearly on the press credentials that I was given while working a college internship.) In lieu of a first-person interview with Aaron, I relied heavily on his quotes gleaned from the historical record, most of them from his *I Had a Hammer* and *Aaron* (originally written with Furman Bisher in 1968 and revised in 1974) autobiographies.

To fully understand Aaron's accomplishments, they must be put in their historical context; Aaron was born and grew up in a different America than exists today. Major league baseball history is distorted by the segregated past of the United States, which had a dramatic effect on Aaron's life and career.

Anyone endeavoring to tell a story like Hank Aaron's owes a tremendous debt to the historians, chroniclers, and researchers who have dug deep to unearth the buried history of his early professional experience in the Negro Leagues. The statistical information on the brief period of time Aaron spent as a member of the Indianapolis Clowns of the Negro American League is particularly difficult to uncover and most likely was even harder to find in years past. Aaron's emotional response to this pivotal period in his life is much more widely recorded in first-hand accounts related by Aaron himself to various journalists and biographers.

At the time of it's first publication in 1970, Robert Peterson's *Only the Ball Was White*, was the first definitive chronicle of the black baseball experience from the post–Civil War Reconstruction Period to Jackie Robinson's breaking of baseball's color barrier in 1947. Peterson's tome is still considered one of the most comprehensive reference books on the topic and has been repeatedly cited as a primary source in most of the historical volumes and accounts of Negro League baseball that followed. Ken Burns and Geoffrey C. Ward's 1994 PBS television documentary film, *Baseball*, and its companion volume also comprise a significant contribution to the canon of historical Negro Leagues reference materials. Including Jim Riley's *Biographical Encyclopedia of the Negro Baseball Leagues*, each of these volumes were relied on heavily to produce the following information and provide a much more complete historical record of what is only covered briefly here. I owe a great debt of gratitude to author-historian Jim Riley, who accepted countless calls, from early morning to late at night and all hours in between. In each and every instance, Jim took his time and patiently helped me piece together the string of events from the first incidents of institutionalized segregation in professional baseball to Jackie Robinson's breakthrough and Aaron's debut.

Most baseball history books include thanks to the National Baseball Hall of Fame and its A. Bartlett Giamatti Research Center. Of particular assistance above and beyond the call of duty was Reference Librarian Claudette Burke, who also became a close personal friend in the process. Many other members of the library staff also found the answers to questions and promptly returned calls.

Gratitude is also extended to Greg Schwalenberg of Baltimore, first, for continually providing encouragement and presenting opportunities, and Norman Macht, second, for assisting in the outlining of chapters which helped make the project seem like a less daunting task.

In no particular order, much thanks also to Atlanta Braves PR Director Jim Schultz, the rest of the Braves media-relations staff, and the Baltimore Orioles PR staff for helping arrange interviews. Thanks to baseball people who allowed me to interview them: Roland Hemond, Dusty Baker, Carla Koplin, Joe Torre, Bob Uecker, Marty Brennaman, Don Baylor, Brooks Robinson, Lou Klimchock, and Johnny Logan. Special thanks to President Jimmy Carter and the Carter Center in Atlanta, Georgia, for his gracious response to a request for a quote. Thanks to David Woodward at the Library of Congress in Washington, D.C. for unearthing early articles on Aaron in the Negro Leagues and early minor league career. Thanks to author Rob Pendell, who if not for a serendipitous meeting with, I would not have been given the opportunity to write this book.

Thanks to friends: Richie Fuller for countless hours of library research and Liz Malby, Bob Cohn, Gary Cieradkowski, Ricky Hemerle for taking time out of their own busy schedules to help with research. Thanks of course to my family and folks for their support.

And finally, thanks to editor John Wagner for constantly providing constructive criticism and helping me streamline the story.

CHRONOLOGY

1934 Henry Louis Aaron is born to parents Estella and Herbert Aaron on February 5.

1942 Aaron family moves to Toulminville, Alabama, just outside of Mobile city limits.

1947 Jackie Robinson of the Brooklyn Dodgers becomes the first African American to play major league baseball on April 15.

1948 Aaron is present when Jackie Robinson visits Mobile and speaks at an auditorium on Davis Avenue.

1950 Aaron plays semiprofessional baseball as shortstop for the Mobile Black Bears.

1952 After being discovered on the Mobile sandlots by scout Ed Scott, Aaron signs a contract calling for $200 a month and $2 per day meal money to play shortstop for the Indianapolis Clowns of the Negro American League.

1952 Before the Negro American League season is over, Aaron is discovered by Boston Braves scout Dewey Griggs. Clowns owner Syd Pollock sells Aaron's contract to the Braves for what eventually amounts to $10,000. Aaron is assigned to the Braves Northern League farm club in Eau Claire, Wisconsin, and receives a hike in pay to $350 a month. Before the next season the Braves will move to Milwaukee.

1953   Together with Jacksonville teammates Horace Garner and Felix Mantilla, Aaron is among the first group of black players to integrate the South Atlantic League. Despite his 36 errors in the field, Aaron leads the league in hitting (.362) and RBIs (125), capturing the league MVP award.

1953   At the end of the season, Aaron marries Barbara Lucas of Jacksonville, Florida, and the pair travel to Puerto Rico where Aaron plays winter ball for Caguas and begins his conversion to an outfielder.

1954   Bobby Thomson's broken ankle is Aaron's big break as he becomes the Braves starting left fielder, filling in for the newly acquired veteran. Aaron connects for his first home run off Vic Raschi on April 13 and his season ends the way Thomson's started—Aaron breaks his ankle while sliding into third base on September 5.

1955   Wearing a new number (44) on his uniform, Aaron hits 27 home runs, drives in 106, and bats .314 in 153 games.

1956   Aaron wins his first batting crown, leading the National League with a .326 average.

1957   With his eleventh-inning home run on September 23, Aaron lifts the Braves to the National League pennant. Aaron is the National League MVP, leading the lead in home runs (44), RBIs (132), and runs scored (118). The Braves defeat the New York Yankees in seven games in the 1957 World Series.

1958   Although his home run (30) and RBI (95) totals drop from the previous year, Aaron helps the Braves to a second National League pennant; however, Milwaukee loses the World Series in seven games to the New York Yankees.

1959   Hitting a career-best .355, Aaron wins his second batting title.

1960   Aaron knocks his 200th home run on July 3 off Ron Kline of the St. Louis Cardinals. Aaron leads the National League in RBIs with 126.

1962   Aaron's brother Tommie joins the Braves and becomes Hank's roommate on the road.

1963   Aaron leads the National League in home runs (44), RBIs (130), and runs scored (121).

1965   In a *Sport* magazine article, Aaron publicly proclaims that black players should be given consideration as managers.

1966   The Braves move to Atlanta, sending Aaron to play most of the remainder of his career in the Deep South. Aaron leads the National League in home runs (44) and RBIs (127).

1967   Aaron speaks out in a *Jet* magazine article entitled "Aaron Blasts Racism in Baseball." Aaron leads the National League in home runs (39) and runs scored (113).

1968   Aaron hits his 500th homer on July 4.

1969   In the first year of divisional format, the Braves win the National League West pennant but lose to the New York Mets in the first National League Championship Series. Aaron hits a home run in each of the three games of the series.

1970   Aaron collects his 3,000th hit on May 17 and is divorced from wife Barbara in December.

1971   On April 27, Aaron connects off San Francisco's Gaylord Perry for his 600th home run.

1973   Aaron marries Atlanta television talk show host Billye Williams.

1974   Aaron ties Babe Ruth's career home-run record of 714 on April 4 with a first-inning blast off Jack Billingham on Opening Day in Cincinnati. Four days later, Aaron hits number 715 off Los Angeles Dodgers pitcher Al Downing in the Braves home opener in Atlanta. At the end of the season, Aaron is traded by the Braves to the Milwaukee Brewers.

1976   Aaron hits the final home run of his career in Milwaukee off California Angels pitcher Dick Drago, setting his all-time record at 755.

1977   Aaron is hired as the Atlanta Braves director of player development.

1982   Aaron is inducted into the National Baseball Hall of Fame on August 1.

1989   The Atlanta Braves name Aaron senior vice president and assistant to the president.

1999   The Hank Aaron Award is created to honor the best overall hitter in the National and American Leagues.

2004   With $76.6 million in sales, Aaron's auto dealerships lead *Black Enterprise* magazine to name Aaron the magazine's "Auto Dealer of the Year." Aaron speaks out on the steroid scandal affecting major league baseball.

INTRODUCTION

If ever someone was properly born into a place and time to fulfill a specific destiny, Hank Aaron, who was born on February 5, 1934, one day before Babe Ruth's 39th birthday, appears to be such a person. Conducting research on Hank Aaron is relatively easy. In most baseball anthologies or reference books with an index, "Aaron, (Henry) Hank" is the first listing, followed by a comparatively long list of page numbers referencing his many accomplishments and contributions to the game. Top of the list is a fitting place for major league baseball's all-time home-run king. Equally appropriate is his listing in the *Baseball Encyclopedia*, where he is first among approximately 15,000 entries, (in 2004 Giants pitcher David Aardsma became the first player listed on the all-time roster) including anyone who has appeared in even one major league game. It's been that way since the first edition of baseball's statistical tome was issued in 1969, with Henry Aaron appearing just ahead of his brother and fellow big leaguer Tommie Aaron. But on the day of Aaron's birth, no one would have thought that he, or any African American, would even appear in any book on major league baseball.

In 1934, the mythical Babe Ruth was already a living legend. Every home run that he hit after his 137th in 1921 set a new all-time major league record, until he retired with a total of 714 after the 1935 season. When Aaron was a child, it was preposterous to believe anyone would ever approach Ruth's records or eclipse his shining star, but that is just what Henry Aaron did forty years later.

Aaron's epic journey from the sandlots of Alabama to the mountaintop of major league baseball's most hallowed record seems even more improbable when one considers that he was born an African American child at a time when full-grown African American men were still excluded from the self-proclaimed "National Pastime." This exclusion was difficult for young Aaron to understand. Like any child with an imagination, he saw himself fulfilling numerous fantasies. When he saw airplanes flying overhead he'd tell his older brother Herbert Jr. that he wanted to be a pilot. Herbert would shake his head and explain to Henry that there were no black pilots. It was the same with baseball, but as well as Aaron could play he could only envision himself as a big leaguer.

In the 1930s, the only profession outlet for African American baseball players were the Negro Leagues, which was formed in 1920 by black baseball players frustrated by the unavailability to them of the major leagues. The first eight teams of this professional Negro circuit set up shop in Kansas City, Indianapolis, Dayton, Detroit, and St. Louis, with two teams in Chicago and a nomadic club calling itself the Cuban Giants.

Aaron's birthplace of Mobile, Alabama, had already in 1934 served notice to the baseball world in the gangly form of Satchel Paige, who was born in Mobile almost thirty years before Aaron and by the 1930s had established himself as the greatest gate attraction in Negro League history. In 1933, Paige teamed with Josh Gibson, who was the slugging equivalent to Paige and of equally legendary stature. Gibson began his career as a surprisingly powerful teenage slugger with the Homestead Grays in 1929. By 1933, he had moved to the Pittsburgh Crawfords and established himself among the game's premier sluggers. In the divided baseball circles of the time, Gibson was known to some as "the Black Babe Ruth," while to others knew Ruth as "the White Josh Gibson." It is estimated that Gibson hit as many as 962 home runs in his 17-year career, with single season marks as high as 69 in 1934, 75 in 1931, and 84 in 1936. Born in Pittsburgh, Gibson could envy the Pittsburgh Pirates heroes of his youth but he could not dream of playing alongside them.

It could conceivably have been the same for young Hank Aaron as he learned to love the game of baseball as a child. Although the exploits of Negro League players were not as well chronicled or reported, Josh Gibson was a hero to aspiring young black ballplayers whose big league dreams were thwarted by segregation. But Mobile was far removed from the northeastern cities that were the central locations of professional black baseball and Aaron claims to have had no knowledge of Gibson at the time of his youth and no heroes among the ranks of the Negro Leagues: "How the hell was I supposed to have a hero? There were no blacks in baseball. Have you ever seen a picture of Babe Ruth surrounded by black kids?"[1]

By the late 1930s, however, African American athletes were beginning to achieve more recognition. Through barnstorming tours and exhibitions against major league teams, news spread of the undeniable talents of players like Gibson and Paige. Black athletes excelled in other sports as well. Jesse Owens' performance in the 1936 Berlin Olympics and Joe Louis' heavyweight boxing championship served notice that black athletes in the United States were indeed to be taken seriously.

While Owens' performance was appreciated by both American citizens back home and in attendance at the Berlin games, the ruling Nazi party opposed his very presence at the games and the debunking of their theories of Aryan supremacy that he represented. Back in the United States, Owens' spectacular achievement elicited an emotional response that prompted national pride in American citizens who were more offended by the particular form of racism practiced in Nazi Germany than by the "separate but equal" type exercised in the United States.

By 1937, the most prominent black athlete in America was heavyweight boxing champion Joe Louis, the first African American officially recognized by the sport's sanctioning bodies since Jack Johnson. Johnson's great success in the early 1900s prompted the search for a "Great White Hope" and led eventually to the adoption by boxing of the same type of type of segregation practiced in baseball, with separate titles awarded to white and black champions. Louis' popularity was fueled by the same wartime nationalism associated with Owens and reached its pinnacle when he defeated German world heavyweight champion Max Schmeling in June 1938. Louis was cast by the media as an American hero defending not only his title but America itself, while Schmeling was portrayed as a symbol of the Nazi regime.

To the black community Louis was even more than an American hero. Many years later Aaron recalled what Louis and his legacy meant to him as a child.

> Growing up in Mobile, Alabama, I didn't really know who Joe Louis was. If he had walked into our neighborhood, probably nobody on my block would have known who he was. We didn't even know what he looked like. But we knew he was something special. In those days before Jackie Robinson integrated baseball, Joe Louis was the only sports hero we had.[2]

While the 1930s was a difficult decade in which to be born for an African American who aspired to the major leagues, time was on Aaron's side. Far more fortunate than the previous generation of black ballplayers or even those just ten years older, Aaron was still only 13 when a bright ray of hope and possibility appeared in the form of Jackie Robinson. It was only when Robinson signed his first minor league contract on October 23, 1945, that Aaron could feasibly fathom becoming a big leaguer. And, in 1947, when Robinson became major league baseball's first black player, young Aaron had an answer for those who would tell him what he could dream and not dream of becoming: "The day Jackie Robinson came to town in 1948, I skipped shop class to hear him speak in the auditorium on Davis Avenue. That same day, I told my father I would be in the big leagues before Jackie retired."[3]

Six years later, Aaron fulfilled his prophecy, reaching the major leagues three years before Robinson's retirement. Aaron's team, the Milwaukee Braves, barnstormed with Robinson's Brooklyn Dodgers as the two teams traveled north after spring training of Aaron's rookie season in 1954. Making stops in southern cities like New Orleans, Memphis, Louisville, and Mobile, where, with his family in attendance, Aaron connected for a single and a double against Robinson's Dodgers. During the time that their careers overlapped, Aaron and Robinson's teams battled through closely contested National League pennant races. The Braves finished just behind the Dodgers in 1954, 1955, and 1956, before capturing the pennant in 1957, Robinson's first year away from the game.

Although Robinson broke through baseball's racial barrier six years before Aaron's big league debut, many analogies can be drawn between their collective experiences as pioneering African American athletes and public figures. While Robinson's and Aaron's contributions to baseball history loom large and remain vivid, the roles they played in moving the country towards its democratic ideals of equality and the acceleration of civil rights for African Americans and other ethnic minority groups make an even greater contribution to American history. Ultimately, both Robinson's and Aaron's stories are more about race relations in America than they are about baseball. If the game and business of baseball prefers to regard itself as the "National Pastime," representative of the country's values and priorities, then it does so for better or worse. While Aaron's heroic accomplishments on the playing field are demonstrative of the realization of the American dream, the exclusion, segregation, bigotry, and hatred he was forced to endure along the way were an American nightmare that he shared with a specific portion of American society.

Throughout Aaron's 23-year career, this dichotomy would be on display throughout the United States and its ballparks. By 1964, when President Lyndon Johnson signed the Civil Rights Bill into law, all sixteen major league teams were manned with African American or black Latin American players. Baseball was well ahead of most of the country in providing opportunities for minorities. Some of baseball's best players were among this pioneering group; many would become perennial All-Stars and Hall-of-Famers, including Roberto Clemente, Frank Robinson, Willie McCovey, Billy Williams, Maury Wills, Orlando Cepeda, Bob Gibson, Dick Allen, and Willie Stargell. However, simply being on a major league baseball team did not necessarily mean equality for black and white players. Every member of this list of luminaries was forced to endure indignities that their white teammates would observe but never experience. In addition to verbal baiting and taunting from fans, opposing players, and even teammates, black players were also subject to racism and segregation in many forms. Black players stayed in separate hotels, ate at separate restaurants, used separate forms of transportation, drank from separate water fountains, and used separate bathrooms.

Aaron was only too familiar with this type of prejudice; he had dealt with it first hand throughout his time in the minor leagues and during the early part of his major league career. He was often not allowed to eat in the same restaurants or stay in the same hotels as his white teammates. By 1964, Aaron had appeared in ten consecutive All Star Games, making the National League team in every season he played with the exception of his rookie year.

In 1966, the Milwaukee Braves moved to Atlanta becoming the first major league team to play in the Deep South and prompting future President Jimmy Carter to say that "Racially integrated sports teams brought about racial integration in the South."[4] Aaron's consistent success, including the league leading 44 home runs and 400th long ball of his career hit during the Braves inaugural season in Atlanta, certainly contributed to the popularity of baseball in Georgia and the acceleration of integration. In 1967, *Jet* magazine ran a cover story with the accompanying headline "Aaron Blasts Racism in Baseball."

On April 3, 1968, Dr. Martin Luther King Jr. delivered his "I've Been to the Mountaintop" speech, in Memphis, Tennessee. The next day King was assassinated. "We had to carry on without our leader," said Aaron of that tragedy.[5] It was a feeling Aaron would revisit a few years later when Jackie Robinson died. Aaron claimed that he felt a sense of responsibility when Robinson retired to use the public forum afforded to him by baseball for the advancement of not just black ballplayers but a generation of all minority groups in need of a voice. "As I said goodbye to Jackie," said Aaron, "I felt like it was my responsibility to keep his dreams alive."[6]

It seemed ever more apparent that Aaron was indeed chosen for the task of not just toppling a legend but of bringing baseball and the country to new frontiers. As his stature increased as a ballplayer, he used the opportunity to speak out on issues he considered more important than baseball while still breaking the most significant records in the game.

Aaron tied Babe Ruth's mark of 714 home runs on April 4, 1974, which happened to be the sixth anniversary of Dr. King's assassination. On the eve of what was Opening Day in Cincinnati, Aaron asked the Reds front office for a moment of silence in King's honor. The request was either denied or ignored. But, as Aaron later recalled, "If nothing else . . . I got the message across that we should be more concerned with Dr. King's legacy than with Babe Ruth's. I was doing my best to keep things in perspective."[7]

At the time, Aaron was the physical embodiment of a generation of African American major leaguers and best exemplified the potential for accomplishment that could be realized when presented with opportunity. Like Ruth's magnetic personality, Aaron's new legacy extended beyond the arena of the playing field. Aaron's accomplishments made a case for what baseball and America could be at their best.

Throughout his career, Aaron maintained a level of consistency that allowed him to close in on the home-run record without drawing much attention to it until he was almost there. Aaron never hit as many as 50 home runs in a single season, reaching a high of 47 only once. To reach Aaron's record of 755 home runs requires hitting an average of 35 home runs a year for 20 years and then 55 home runs more. Aaron also holds the records for runs batted in (2,297) and total bases (6,856), a number that may be better understood when compared to his closest follower, Stan Musial at 6,134.

As a standout African American player and one whose home team played in the Deep South, Aaron was the man chosen to inherit the mantle of using baseball to champion the cause of civil rights. This fact became increasingly evident when the eyes of the world were focused on him as he closed in on the home-run record in 1974. Aaron, said former Atlanta Mayor, Maynard Jackson, was "A man big enough for the job."[8]

NOTES

1. Phil Musick, *Hank Aaron: The Man Who Beat the Babe* (New York: Associated Features Inc., 1974), 122.

2. Joe Garner, *And The Crowd Goes Wild* (Naperville, IL: Sourcebooks, 1999), ix.

3. Henry Aaron, with Lonnie Wheeler, *I Had a Hammer* (New York: HarperCollins Publishers, 1991), 14.

4. Mike Tollin, *Hank Aaron, Chasing the Dream* (TBS Productions, 1995). Documentary film.

5. Ibid.

6. Ibid.

7. Aaron and Wheeler, *I Had a Hammer,* 262.

8. Tollin, *Chasing the Dream.*

In his post-baseball career, Aaron has excelled as a businessman and entrepreneur. In 2004 *Black Enterprise* magazine named Aaron its Auto Dealer of the Year. *National Baseball Hall of Fame Library, Cooperstown, N.Y.*

An Alabama Childhood, 1934–1947

As Hank Aaron was entering the world in Mobile, Alabama, on February 5, 1934, Babe Ruth was bed-ridden with a case of influenza at his Riverside Drive apartment on New York City's Upper West Side. One day shy of his thirty-ninth birthday (which at the time Ruth believed was his fortieth), it was already shaping into a bad year for the Bambino. With the whole country deep in the throws of the Great Depression, Ruth, for the second straight season, reluctantly agreed to a dramatic cut in pay. In 1933, the Babe saw his salary cut from $75,000 to $52,000, which was further trimmed to $35,000 for 1934. On the day of Aaron's birth, Ruth's days with the Yankees were numbered and a changing of the guard was at hand. A thousand miles to the south the next home run king had arrived.

In 1934, Mobile, Alabama, and the south were so different from New York that they might as well have been a different country. Mobile was a rural outpost a few years shy of a population surge that would be fueled by a migration of farm workers looking for city work. While racial segregation was still the norm across the Deep South, where basically Black and White America co-existed as almost separate countries, Mobile had earned a reputation, dating back to the 1920s, of being slightly ahead of the curve regarding race relations and racial politics. In the 1930s, years before the Civil Rights movement gained any momentum, a postal worker named John LeFlore, who had been involved in an altercation with a white person trying to keep him off a city bus, formed a Mobile chapter of the NAACP. Even before the Civil War, Mobile's Spring Hill private college was an integrated institution. The Mobile Public Library was available to blacks well before the same was true in most other southern cities. But despite this relatively liberal climate, segregation was still a part of life in Mobile and existed mainly as a socioeconomic condition.

Poor blacks lived in areas inhabited by families whose fathers worked as ship builders or on the docks in seaport towns like Down the Bay, where Herbert and Estella Aaron had relocated from the town of Camden in Wilcox County, near Selma. Before moving to Down the Bay to find factory work, Herbert broke the family's chain of preachers by choosing instead to labor in the cotton fields. Although many businesses in Down the Bay were laying off more employees than they were hiring, Herbert eventually found work as a boilermaker's helper on the dry docks, building and repairing navy ships for about seventy-five dollars a week. Until there were too many children to take care of at home, Estella worked in one of Mobile's white households, where work was available for blacks as maids and cooks.

Henry was Herbert and Estella's third child, after older sister Sarah and older brother Herbert Jr. By the time Hank was four years old, he was following the bigger kids to Council Field and was already showing a prowess for baseball. Many years later Mobile policeman Ted Blunt would remember glimpsing the young Aaron. "[E]ven then," recalled Blunt, "Henry threw a baseball like a man, not a little child."[1]

Whether he was playing pickup games with older children or makeshift games of his own, the baseball bug bit Aaron at a tender age. "I had a taste for it in my mouth that never went away," said Aaron.[2] Given rag balls that were put together by his father or nylon hose wrapped around golf balls of his own design, Aaron was incessantly playing games of catch with friends or part of the family's home.

"I could spend hours hitting a ball with a stick or throwing it on the roof and hitting it or catching it when it came down. I was so good at rolling that ball up on the roof that I could toss it over the house and run around and catch it before it hit the ground on the other side," Aaron remembered.[3]

When Hank was eight, the Aaron family moved to the rural neighborhood of Toulminville just outside the Mobile city limits, where the wide open spaces provided ample room for young Hank and his new friends to play pickup games at a moment's notice. Aaron and his pals cleared a vacant lot near his home that was formerly a pecan grove and drew up their own baseball diamond. A few years later, when the city of Mobile officially annexed Toulminville, Carver Park was created on that same site as the first officially designated recreational area for blacks in Mobile. "It was like having Ebbets Field in my backyard. I'd be over there every day after school and in the summer, usually with my neighbor, Cornelius Giles, and anybody else who could get out of his chores," Aaron later recalled.[4]

Because Mobile produced many excellent baseball players during his generation, Aaron believed Carver Park might have been a primary reason. A black recreational league was formed drawing teams to Carver Park from all the black neighborhoods in the surrounding area. The loosely organized league kept standings and rivalries developed between neighborhoods like Down the Bay and Toulminville. Over the years, future black major league Hall-of-Famers like Willie McCovey and Billy Williams, and big leaguers like Cleon Jones, Tommie Agee, and Aaron's younger brother Tommie, all had roots in Mobile.

Even before Aaron's appearance, Mobile was a hotbed for baseball talent. Satchel Paige was also from Down the Bay, where he pitched for semipro black teams as a teenager and worked out with the white Mobile Bears of the Southern League at Hartwell Field in the early 1920s, before embarking on his negro league career in 1926. Ted "Double Duty" Radcliffe, nicknamed for his abilities as both pitcher and catcher, and his brother Alex, were also established Negro League stars born in Mobile.

In addition to the white minor league teams and black semipro teams, major league clubs would stop to play exhibition games at Hartwell Field on their way north after spring training in Florida. Despite the limited amount of time Aaron spent in this part of Mobile, memories of the place, vague as they may be, were passed to him in the form of stories told to him by Herbert. Writing later in his *I Had a Hammer* autobiography, Aaron recalled his father's account of a big league exhibition: "My father climbed a tree to see Babe Ruth play at Hartwell Field in 1928, and he swears he saw Ruth hit a ball into the coal car of a train and they didn't retrieve the ball until the train pulled into New Orleans."[5]

Named for his paternal grandfather, a farmer and preacher whose presence remained constant throughout his life, Aaron attributed some of his own personality traits to his grandfather's influence. "People in my family say that I'm like Papa Henry in a lot of ways—deliberate and good at making decisions. I hope I picked up a few things from him, because he was a wise man. Papa Henry could see things that nobody else could see. He believed that his religion helped him look into the future, and he always predicted that Daddy's family would somehow be known forever. I don't know if he was talking about me, but I like to think that I made his prediction come true."[6]

Aaron's improbable future and informal introduction to the game involved hitting bottle caps with a broomstick, held with a cross-handed grip. He created one-on-one skill games with his childhood friend Cornelius Giles, competing to see who could send the bottle caps a greater distance. He might not have realized it at the time but he was developing a distinctive style of hitting off his front foot with a quick snap of the wrists that would become his hallmark. Later, when he traded in his broomsticks and bottle caps for bats and balls, this swing would produce bullet-like line drives.

"When I look back on my life, I can see that all through my childhood I was being prepared to play baseball. Whether you call it luck or fate or chance, it took one coincidence after another to get me to the big leagues, as if somebody or something was up there mapping it all out for me. Being born in Mobile was my first break, and moving to Toulminville was the second."[7]

Toulminville was a small rural village just past the edge of Mobile's city limits. When Henry was eight years old, his family moved from Mobile into a six-bedroom house built on a pair of abandoned and overgrown lots. Herbert Aaron Sr. paid $110 for the lots and $100 for a couple of carpenters to build the house.

There was no running water or electricity in the Aarons' home; they took water from a nearby well and the "bathroom" was an outhouse. With eight children to feed, the family would often subsist for many weeks on a consistent diet of cornbread, butter beans, and collard greens.

"We were practically vegetarians before we ever heard the word," Aaron later recalled. "You can believe the Aaron kids didn't have any fat on them. My sister Gloria was so skinny that I called her Neck Bone. My brother Tommie's nickname was Pork Chop, because he always wanted one. We all described ourselves as six o'clock—straight up and down."[8]

Herbert Aaron found himself unemployed as often as not and doubled as a moonshiner to make ends meet. Alongside the house, Herbert created his own bar, called the Black Cat Inn, which was just about the only tavern in town serving the African American community. As soon as they were old enough, every member of the family chipped in and did a lot of the work together. Hank's oldest sister, Sarah, helped run the tavern. His older brother, Herbert Jr., worked for a woman who owned the local grocery store and acted almost as another mother for the Aaron children in the tight-knit community where neighbors treated each other like family.

By his own admission, Hank was not the hardest worker in the family, losing jobs almost as quickly as he obtained them, opting instead to find a pickup game of baseball or create some form of the game he could play by himself. "I suppose you could say I was a lazy kid and a smart kid," Hank said. "I was lazy as far as doing chores around the house, but smart when it came to playing baseball and other sports. This is what I really wanted to do even when I was eleven or twelve years old."[9]

Perhaps the most significant job of his adolescent years was delivering blocks of ice. Years later in a bit of manufactured folklore, Aaron would tell reporters that he developed the great strength in his wrists by carrying twenty-five-pound chunks of ice up flights of stairs with a pair of tongs. However, he later discredited his own story, citing that he lost the job rather quickly after a driving mishap and doubted that it had any serious impact on his muscular development. The story has been told and retold and exaggerated in numerous written accounts to the point where Hank carried fifty-pound blocks of ice up three or more flights of stairs. This type of truth stretching was a playful habit of Aaron's early in his professional career.

It was the same playful nature that kept Aaron from actively pursuing employment or even an education as a kid, primarily concerning himself with baseball, with which he was completely enraptured. And it was evident even at this early stage in his development that Aaron was a standout player.

Between Aaron's home and the neighborhood baseball diamond was a field of tall corn that Hank had beaten a path through. "You'd see his head bobbing up and down over that corn, and in a few seconds everybody knew that Henry was coming. And whoever was batting for our team, he would just lay that bat down on the ground, because Henry was going to pinch-hit," said Robert Driscoll, a childhood friend of Aaron's.[10]

Such was Aaron's stature as a player that even as a youngster his peers held him in reverence. "If he wasn't there it actually wasn't a game," Cornelius Giles later recalled during an interview for a television documentary.[11] Thus, by the time Aaron reached his early teens, he was already recognized as an exceptional baseball player, and playing baseball was already his chosen career path.

NOTES

1. Phil Musick, *Hank Aaron: The Man Who Beat the Babe* (New York: Associated Features Inc., 1974), 31.
2. Ibid.
3. Henry Aaron, with Lonnie Wheeler, *I Had a Hammer* (New York: HarperCollins Publishers, 1991), 11.
4. Ibid.
5. Ibid., 14.
6. Ibid., 17.
7. Ibid., 11.
8. Ibid., 9.
9. Joel H. Cohen, *Hammerin' Hank of the Braves* (New York: Scholastic Book Services, 1973), 11.
10. Mike Tollin, *Hank Aaron, Chasing the Dream* (TBS Productions, 1995). Documentary film.
11. Ibid.

Aaron follows the trajectory of his historic 715th home run on April 8, 1974 at Fulton County Stadium in Atlanta. *National Baseball Hall of Fame Library, Cooperstown, N.Y.*

BIG LEAGUE DREAMS,
1947–1951

If the *Macmillan Baseball Encyclopedia* is considered the "Bible of major league baseball," then the period before 1947 reflected in this book can be called the "Old Testament." The sweeping changes brought about by Jackie Robinson's entry into the major leagues announced the arrival of baseball's new age. This new age would be characterized at first by the availability of opportunity to an increasing number of ballplayers, and later by an increasing number of places to play and better means of getting there. Expansion and rapid transportation brought the game to new frontiers, literally and figuratively. However, Jackie Robinson's signing with the Dodgers did not exactly open up the floodgates to other black players. It was more of a slow trickle, like a small hole in the dyke that a white finger kept plugged up; it took more than another full decade before the pressure for integration on both major and minor league baseball was too strong to hold back. Hank Aaron would be among the chosen few given the task of integrating leagues that had operated under Jim Crow rules of segregation for decades.

The day Robinson came to Mobile is the beginning of Aaron's coming of age story. It is the point in time when Aaron made his mental commitment to baseball above all else. Aaron was a 14-year-old aspiring ballplayer when Jackie Robinson stopped in Mobile on a barnstorming trip as the Brooklyn Dodgers made their way north after spring training in Florida. Young Henry cut out of school that day to hear Jackie speak in an auditorium on Davis Avenue on the border of Mobile and the rural village of Toulminville that Aaron called home. Later that same afternoon, Aaron watched with his father from the colored section of the seats when Jackie played in an exhibition game at Hartwell Field.

Although he played a lot of sandlot baseball with his Toulminville friends, Aaron played more softball than baseball until he was a teenager. In the Deep South, with the exception of maybe Mobile, baseball also took a back seat to football, with universities like Alabama, Auburn, and Louisiana State University (LSU) garnering a lion's share of the attention of—especially white—southern sports fans. When Aaron enrolled at Mobile's Central High, his mother preferred that he play football, hoping it might provide him with a college scholarship. Aaron, however, did not want anything pulling him away from baseball. Thus Aaron's foray into football was brief and pursued more as a means of attracting a romantic interest and not because of any affinity for the sport. Nonetheless, despite his disinterest and his relatively diminutive stature, Aaron played football well enough to be offered a scholarship by Florida A&M.

Central High did not have a baseball team but Aaron played catcher, pitcher, and infield for its fast-pitch softball team, where his prodigious blasts served notice of his potential. By his own estimation, he hit many home runs on a field without a fence, a fact requiring him to hurry around the bases. His raw and unrefined skills included running on his heels and batting cross-handed (with his left hand on top, wrong for a right-handed hitter). "We were never told the right way to bat and we didn't lose any sleep over technique," Aaron recalled.[1]

As he became increasingly fascinated and obsessed with baseball, Aaron's disinterest in school accelerated accordingly, reaching a point where he had basically ceased attending class. A typical day would have Hank going through the motions of going to school. To fool his parents, he would wake up and leave the house at the appropriate hour. He would head in the direction of Central High, maybe actually walk into the building, and then out the back door to Davis Avenue where he would waste away the morning hours at the local pool hall. In the afternoon, he would listen to the Brooklyn Dodgers or any other baseball game broadcast over the radio. Aaron decided that school had nothing left to offer him because by this time he knew he was going to be a ballplayer. Among the most popular and published quotes attributed to Aaron concerning this period of his life explains his rationale: "I want to be a baseball player, and I'll learn more about playing second base listening to Jackie Robinson play on the radio than I will in school."[2]

Aaron described his morning ritual of bypassing school for pool as a means of killing time in a safe haven where nobody would question why he was there until the game came on. During one extended leave of absence from school lasting approximately 40 days by own Aaron's estimate, he was expelled from school but did not tell his parents and continued to pretend to be going to school each day. Eventually Henry was found out by his father. Herbert walked into the pool hall during the middle of a weekday afternoon and caught his teenage son with his hand wrapped around a pool cue when he it should have been holding a pencil in school.

Herbert motioned towards Henry that it was time to follow him home. When they got there the two sat in a broken down family car parked in front of the Aaron home, and had one of the most lengthy and memorable father and son chats of Henry's life. While Henry reiterated that he was intent on being a professional ballplayer, Herbert insisted that it would not come at the expense of school. Using himself as an example, the father explained to the son how at the same age he was not afforded the opportunity to continue his formal education in school, having instead to work to pay his way through life. He reminded Henry of the fifty cents he gave him each day to buy lunch at school, while he only took a quarter for himself—Henry's education was more important to Herbert than his own hunger. Aaron later recalled that this talk went on for two hours before a compromise was reached. It was decided that Henry would transfer to the Josephine Allen Institute, a private school, at the beginning of the new school year in the upcoming fall season.

In the meantime, Henry worked at various part-time jobs and played as much softball and baseball as possible. During the Mobile recreational league games, Henry was discovered by Ed Scott, the manager of a local semipro team called the Mobile Black Bears. Most of the players on the Black Bears club were grown men who worked during the week and played baseball on Sundays as a means of earning extra income. Despite Henry's younger age and smaller size, Scott saw something in Aaron that made him believe the youngster could play with grown men. Scott asked Henry if he would like to play for the Black Bears, but young Aaron was reluctant to entertain Scott's overtures. As much as he wanted to play ball, he knew his mother would be opposed, especially to playing on Sundays.

Scott made repeated visits to the Aaron household asking for Estella's permission to let Henry play for the Black Bears, explaining that he would also be paid for his services. Estella kept telling Scott that she would let Henry play sometime but didn't let him know when that sometime might be. Scott showed up so often that Henry would hide when he came around rather than have to deal with explaining why he couldn't play. Eventually Estella gave in and one day Henry surprised Ed Scott by showing up at Mitchell Field, in the nearby village of Prichard, just prior to the start of a game. He asked if would get a uniform if he joined the team. Scott recounted the day he fitted him out with some flannels and wrote his name at shortstop on the day's lineup card.

"He was only seventeen and the rest of us had wives and children. He was green as he could be. He stood up there at the plate upright, no crouch at all, and the other team figured he wasn't ready. The pitcher tried to get a fastball by him, and he hit a line drive that banged against the old fence they had around the outfield out there—nearly put the ball through the fence. They walked him the rest of the time," remembered Scott.[3] Still batting cross-handed, the shy and scrawny teenager had, in storybook fashion, slain his first dragon.

In addition to the games the Bears played at Mitchell Field, the team was a traveling unit as well, and while Estella allowed Henry to play in the team's home games, even on Sundays, traveling with the team was still out of the question.

Aaron made an immediate impression upon Black Bears owner Ed Tucker, who paid his players ten dollars after every game. While every other player lined up to receive their money on Sundays, Tucker told Henry to come by his home to be paid on Mondays when either he or his wife would then give him an extra couple of dollars. As the story of Aaron's life is told and retold, various autobiographical accounts have him receiving extra money from Tucker once, sometimes, or always. Suffice it to say the Tuckers, who lived in Aaron's Toulminville neighborhood, took a special liking to young Henry.

Unbeknownst to Aaron, his professional initiation as a Sunday shortstop with the Black Bears was also an audition for a prominent position at another level. Besides running the Black Bears for Ed Tucker, Ed Scott moonlighted as a scout for the Indianapolis Clowns of the Negro American League. As Aaron continued to bang balls off the outfield wall, throwing and running with an unrestrained ease and grace that set him apart from the semipro competition, it didn't take long for Scott to realize that his 17-year-old prodigy was bound for broader horizons. Scott arranged for the Bears to play exhibition games with Negro League teams like the Clowns, which in effect served Aaron as tryouts for the opposing team. After one such game in 1951, Bunny Downs, the Clowns business manager, who Scott had played for when Downs was the field manager for the Negro League Norfolk Stars, approached Aaron.

"I don't think I knew what was going on, but I hit the ball hard that day— a home run and maybe a double or two, as I recall—and after the game, Bunny Downs came up and asked me how I'd like to play shortstop for the Clowns," Aaron recalled.[4]

Seeking to seal some kind of deal on the spot while he was in town, Downs went home with Aaron immediately following the game to talk with his parents about the possibility of Henry playing for the Clowns. Herbert and Estella explained to Downs the agreement the family had made regarding Henry's return to school in the fall. Downs said he would wait and send Henry a contract at the conclusion of the school year. Aaron didn't really think he would ever see Downs again. At 17, Aaron was already cynical beyond his years. Although he never doubted his own ability, he was frustrated by the need to simultaneously pursue both his dreams and goals and those of his parents.

Later that summer, the Brooklyn Dodgers held an open tryout for black players in Mobile. Once again, Jackie Robinson was at the forefront of Aaron's consciousness. Jackie was not at the tryout—it was the middle of the season and he was with the Dodgers—but he was present in spirit for Henry and the other hopefuls for whom the Dodgers represented possibility and opportunity. By 1951, in addition to Robinson, the Dodgers had also signed catcher Roy Campanella and pitcher Don Newcombe. For three and a half baseball seasons, Henry had been striving toward his dream of playing with Robinson and when the Dodgers came to town he hoped against hope that it was time to join Jackie in the big leagues. But the tryout was tough, drawing the best talent from Mobile and the surrounding area. Many of Henry's recreation league rivals from Down the Bay were bigger and stronger-looking, and made a better appearance than the still scrawny and cross-handed hitting Henry. They carried themselves with cocksure mannerisms far removed from Aaron's quiet and unassuming demeanor. It was all Henry could do to squeeze his way into the batting cage for a couple of swings before being muscled out by one of the bigger players. One of the Dodgers scouts told him that he was too small and should head home. It was not yet time for Henry and Jackie to play with or against each other. Henry didn't think he got a fair shake that day and the disappointment he felt caused him to break his allegiance as a Dodgers fan. He didn't mind later when he heard the radios coming from storefronts on Davis Avenue as Giants second baseman Bobby Thomson hit the most famous home run in baseball history to beat the Dodgers for the 1951 National League pennant. In fact, it was one of the most inspirational moments in his life, providing him with a picture in his head of teammates carrying him off the field after hitting a similar home run some day. Along with joining Jackie in the majors, it was a scenario he would often imagine and revisit in the future.

As fall turned into winter and Henry continued to struggle even at a new school, his mind wandered back to Bunny Downs and the Indianapolis Clowns. Would they call after the New Year like Downs said they would? He checked the mailbox every day for the contract Downs said he would send, until, one day, it appeared. Clowns owner Syd Pollock offered Aaron $200 a month. If Henry was still interested, he should meet the team at its spring training headquarters in Winston-Salem, North Carolina.

The next hurdle was convincing his parents to let him leave before the school year was up. After much discussion, soul-searching, and yet another contingency deal, Henry was surprised that it was Estella and not Herbert who agreed to let him go. Herbert was still not sold on the idea that $200 a month was worth more than a formal education. Spring training would serve as Henry's tryout for the team; if he made the club he told his mother he would still finish high school in the off-season. If he failed to make the club, he told her not only would he finish high school but he would also go on to college. In the meantime, the $200 a month would be of great assistance to the entire family. To sweeten the pie, the Clowns added a couple of shirts for Henry and a new suit for Herbert. Later Henry recalled that Ed Scott must have received a "little something" for his efforts as well.

A few days later, a skinny scared kid left home for the first time in his life, embarking on a journey that would see him grow into a strong confident man. He would be asked to prove himself repeatedly on an odyssey that would have him chasing down the past and the future, and in so doing paving the way—like Jackie Robinson before him—not just for himself but for others, affording him glimpses of heaven and hell along the way.

NOTES

1. Aaron, with Wheeler, *I Had a Hammer*, 20.
2. Musick, *Hank Aaron*, 34.
3. Aaron, with Wheeler, *I Had a Hammer*, 23.
4. Ibid., 24.

3

TEARS OF A CLOWN, 1952

Although she agreed to let him go, Estella was too distraught to see Henry off at the station the day he left to join the Indianapolis Clowns for spring training in 1952. She stuffed two bucks in his pocket, two sandwiches in a paper sack, a pair of pants in an old suitcase, and struggled to watch through the welling pools in her eyes as Henry drove off with his father, older brother, sister, and Ed Scott to catch his train. Of course, 18-year-old Henry was excited, but it was with mixed emotions that he boarded the train to Winston-Salem, staring long and hard at that most familiar and important group of people fighting back his own tears while they faded into the distance. As the train rolled along he got his first real look at white people and an introduction to the discrimination associated with their presence when he was instructed to stay out of the dining car. He didn't have any money for it anyway. He struggled with the impulse to get off the train at every stop along the way to turn around and head back home.

In addition to the meager belongings Aaron carried with him, Ed Scott had handed Henry an envelope that he was instructed to pass along unopened to Bunny Downs upon his arrival. It would be years before Aaron learned what was written on the piece of paper the envelope contained: "Forget everything about this player. Just watch his bat."[1]

Downs or field manager Buster Haywood were not afforded a whole lot of chances to watch Henry's bat. In the chill of the Winston-Salem spring, Aaron's Clowns teammates turned a cold shoulder to the youngster who would rival them for a job. On windy, cold, and wet days Aaron was not even given a jacket, which was part of the uniform worn by just about all the other players. "They treated me like I was a disease, a new player meant an older one had to go," recalled Aaron.[2]

It was like the Dodgers tryout all over again when he tried to get time in the batting cage—no sooner would he get a few licks in than he was bullied out by one of the veteran big guys. The veterans saw in Aaron something they resented: the potential for greatness and big-league stardom made possible for him not only by the promise of his skills but by the newfound avenue to the majors made available by Jackie Robinson and the end of big-league segregation. Their days, if not all but over, were certainly numbered. Unlike young Henry, Negro League ballplayers in their mid-30s or even late 20s were born a little too soon. As a rookie, Henry was routinely picked on and subjected to ritualistic hazing from the veterans, who poked fun at everything from his size to the condition of his equipment and even his clothing.

Around the batting cages or in the evening at the pool hall located under the team's quarters, veteran players would make light of how much better things would be when they got rid of the kids who would be cut from the team before the season started. Even manager Haywood would join in the conversation talking about the sights they would all see when the team would start traveling around the country and get on with the season's schedule, casting a wink and a sly glance at Henry, who wasn't sure he would be going along. But once again fate intervened. Even though Henry had hardly been given a look during the early workouts and practice sessions, an injury to one of the regular infielders at the start of the exhibition season opened up a spot in the line-up; given the opportunity, Henry quickly displayed his ability.

While playing the infield was not his forte, he distinguished himself at the plate, and soon he developed a reputation for being able to hit the ball where it was pitched. Undisciplined in his approach to the strike zone, Henry was a free swinger, and while the same habit may have been a detriment to other players, in Henry's case it did not matter: he went with outside pitches to the opposite field and smacked line drives off of and over the right field fence; he took golf swings at low balls and lifted them for singles into center field; and he pulled inside pitches with such authority as to frighten opposing third baseman.

His quiet and unassuming demeanor remained unchanged despite his success. While his teammates, opposing players, managers, and scouts took notice, Henry casually carried on with his business, seemingly oblivious to the times when the hot glare of the spotlight fell upon him. It was his nature not to speak a lot, and in the presence of the veteran ballplayers he mostly kept to himself. Thus, at this early point in his life, he began to develop a reputation for nonchalance and even drowsiness that he would carry for the duration of his career.

His penchant for sleeping and his ability to sleep almost anywhere became legendary and were vividly recalled by teammates.

"He fell asleep when he got in that bus in Kansas and I don't think he wake [*sic*] up until we get [*sic*] to Buffalo. Then he get off that bus and get ten hits in eleven times at bat," said a Clowns teammate.[3]

Henry was not in the line-up on the first day of the spring exhibition season in Chattanooga, but he burst on the scene a few days later in Buffalo when Haywood penciled him in for the first game of a double-header against the same Kansas City Monarchs.

In Aaron's first at bat, he knocked the third professional pitch he ever saw onto the street that ran behind the left-field fence of the ballpark in Buffalo. He went 4-for-4 with a pair of doubles and a single and connected for 6 consecutive hits in the second game and had a hand in turning 5 double plays at shortstop.

Now his teammates started looking at each other, instead of him, trying to figure out which one of them would be saying goodbye soon. In a league where talent had been in steady decline for five years, with the best players being funneled to the major leagues, when the regular season got underway the 18-year-old rookie sensation quickly stood out among the rest. Twenty-seven former Negro Leaguers had made it to the major leagues, and many more to Minor League affiliates; these were the best players from the Negro Leagues. The attention drawn to Aaron was due in no small measure to the lobbying efforts of Clowns owner Syd Pollock who regularly sent out press releases on his star players and wrote personal letters to major league farm and scouting directors.

During this period in Negro League history, teams like the Clowns made more money selling their best players to major league organizations than they did at the gate. Among Pollock's favorite potential buyers were the Boston Braves. Pollock's first reference to Aaron came at the end of a letter written to Braves farm director John Mullen. The mention came in the form of this curious little teaser: "P.S. We got an 18-year-old shortstop batting cleanup for us."[4]

It didn't take long for the news of the Clowns young power-hitting shortstop to spread through the scouting grapevine. In addition to the Braves, other big league suitors began lining up, including the New York Giants, who two years earlier had beaten the Braves in a bidding war to procure the services of another young Negro League phenomenon named Willie Mays.

Despite the fact that they were the best team in the Negro American League, having won their division championship the two previous seasons, the Clowns doubled as a traveling carnival act, employing side show entertainers. And they also played a Harlem Globetrotters vaudeville brand of baseball as a means of enhancing attendance. Supposedly hailing from Indianapolis, the team played all its games on the road. It was an example of the steady decline the Negro Leagues were experiencing at the time, after all the best players moved on to the major leagues. However, when it came to Aaron, Syd Pollock was not fooling around. He told Henry he was his drawing card and the Clowns used Aaron's image in promotional posters, giving him top billing over famous Clowns mascots, King Tut and Spec Bebop.

Towards the end of the exhibition game season, the Clowns embarked on a lengthy road trip west heading out from North Carolina to Texas and Oklahoma. Aaron honed his ability to sleep anywhere during the long noisy bus rides because the Clowns would only stay in a hotel one night per week.

A few weeks later, the phone at Aaron's parents' home began to ring with calls from major league scouts and then Ed Scott started calling Henry on the road counseling him on his options from home. Sensing the urgency not to be outdone by the Giants again, the Boston Braves were making serious overtures and were in the process of negotiating the purchase of Aaron's contract from the Clowns.

On the return trip from the Southwest, the Clowns made barnstorming stops in Kansas City, Chattanooga, Knoxville, Nashville, Asheville, and points in between before arriving in Baltimore for the official Negro American League Opening Day against the Philadelphia Stars. The Baltimore *Afro-American* weekly newspaper described the match as follows in its May 17, 1952 edition:

> A group of top-flight stars will lead the nationally famous Indianapolis Clowns into Baltimore Memorial Stadium for their meeting with the Philadelphia Stars on Sunday afternoon, in their official Negro American League opening twin bill here at 2 P.M. The Clowns are the Eastern division champions of the Negro American League. King Tut, funmaker of the Clowns, assisted by pint sized Spec Bebop will also perform. Among the leading talent displaying their wares for the Clowns are Henry (Speed) Merchant, one of the league's top outfielders and base stealers; Ray Neil, the first player signed in the Texas League from the colored ranks and top-ranking second sacker; and newcomer Henry Aaron, youngest shortstop to ever break into the league as a regular.[5]

Aaron went 1-for-4 in the first game and knocked two prodigious blasts in the nightcap, drawing comparisons for the first time with Josh Gibson, comparisons that served as Hank's first lessons in Negro Leagues history.

He was also receiving an eye-opening education on the sociopolitical structure of America in an interactive way that he was sure he would never have learned back at the Josephine Allen Institute in Mobile. A particularly poignant firsthand encounter is forever etched in Aaron's memory: an incident at a restaurant in Washington D.C. on the day following the Baltimore double-header. While waiting out a rain delay that would eventually cancel a pair of games scheduled at Washington's Griffith Stadium, Aaron and his teammates were eating breakfast. At the conclusion of the meal, they could hear plates being broken in the kitchen.

"What a horrible sound. Even as a kid, the irony of it hit me: Here we were in the capital in the land of freedom and equality, and they had to destroy the plates that had touched the forks that had been in the mouths of black men. If dogs had eaten off those plates, they'd have washed them," Aaron has recalled on more than one occasion.[6]

A week later, Braves scout Dewey Griggs caught up with Henry in Buffalo, where the Clowns were playing a double-header with Kansas City. Buffalo was the Clowns home away from home, closer to Syd Pollock's residence in Tarrytown, New York. Aaron impressed Griggs that day, hitting another home run and a couple of base hits in the first game. In between games of the double-header, Griggs approached Aaron with some critical questions concerning his defensive play, particularly his throws to first base. Aaron responded by claiming he was throwing that way because he had not warmed up his arm properly, adding that he didn't even have a jacket. "Get this kid a jacket," Griggs mouthed to anyone and no one in particular, after which Haywood was able to drum one up.[7]

Griggs later delivered his critique of Aaron's performance to Syd Pollock, and stated his concerns over Aaron's cross-handed grip and perceived lack of hustle in running around the bases. Pollock understood that if Griggs was paying this much attention to Aaron, a sale of the young player's contract was not far off, and Pollock became personally involved with sharpening Aaron's skills to make him a more marketable ballplayer. He asked Henry not to hit cross-handed anymore. Sensing he was on the brink of a breakthrough, Aaron, with determined focus, made the adjustments immediately.

> The first time I came to bat after that, I held the bat the right way and hit a home run. I never batted cross-handed again, except for now and then when a tough pitcher had two strikes on me. The next time up, I bunted to show Mr. Griggs that I could run. And whenever they hit a ball to me, I made sure I threw it overhand to first base, as hard as I could. I guess Mr. Griggs was satisfied because he wrote a letter to John Mullen that night.[8]

Griggs' May 25, 1952, letter to Boston Braves General Manager John Mullen concluded with the following paragraph:

On June 15 Indianapolis plays two games with Kansas City at Buffalo and at that time I will give you a complete story on the boy. I am satisfied with the boys [*sic*] hitting. However I want to see him make plays to both to his right and left and slow hit balls that he has to come in after. Also another look at his throwing. This boy could be the answer. —Sincerely yours, Dewey S. Griggs.[9]

Although the letter is obviously flattering in its assessment of Aaron's ability and potential, especially as a hitter, the use of the word boy, three times in one paragraph, carried connotations Aaron was just beginning to deal with and be reminded of continually. Whether racially motivated or not—Aaron was still a teenager—Griggs' use of the word and the use of it by others later in his life still stung Aaron with its racial implications.

"It's so hard," said Aaron to writers Stan Baldwin and Jerry Jenkins for their *Bad Henry* book. "And it takes so long for the average black to be identified as a man. He goes through the early years of his adult life being called 'boy.' Then when he gets to be 40 or 50 years old, he is 'pop.' And after pop comes 'boy' again. It's hard for a black person to know who he is."[10]

Griggs would not make it back to Buffalo on June 15 and neither would Aaron. Just four days after receiving Griggs' letter, on May 29, Mullen wired a telegram to Syd Pollock containing his bid for Aaron's contract. On the same day, Pollock also received a bid for Aaron's services from John Schwarz, secretary of the New York Giants farm clubs. The offers were for similar amounts of money with slightly varying incremental incentives depending on Aaron's successful climb up the organizational ladder. The Braves would pay Henry $350 to play in the minors for its Northern League club at Eau Claire, Wisconsin, and the Clowns would receive $2,500 up front and another $7,500 if the Braves kept him in their organization for a minimum of thirty days. The Giants would keep Aaron's monthly salary at the same $250 he was receiving from Clowns to play for Sunbury, Pennsylvania, of the Interstate League. The Clowns would get the same $2,500 down payment offered by the Braves, another $2,500 if Aaron was promoted to the highest minor league level, and another $7,500 if he made it all the way to the majors and remained on the big club's roster for thirty days. Aaron was aware that if he signed with the Giants he might have had an opportunity to play with Willie Mays, the most recent Negro League player to star in the majors, but he liked the fact that the Braves would pay him a higher salary from the start. He also thought his chances of eventually making it to the big leagues were better with the Braves. Whether it was because he had Henry's best interests at heart or that he was guaranteed more money sooner, Pollock sold Aaron's contract to the Braves even though he could have made more money in the long run had Aaron signed with the Giants.

Ultimately, the choice of which team to sign with was Aaron's to make; over the years he has questioned himself on his decision. His opinion on this topic seems to have changed over the course of time. In his 1974 autobiography, *Aaron,* written with *Atlanta Journal* sportswriter Furman Bisher, he recalled the contract negotiations as follows:

> I was too young to know or care or have any idea about how deals like that were made then, but there are times now that I think about it when I want to kick myself. A Paul Petit [pitching prospect signed by the Pirates at about the same time Aaron signed with the Braves] gets $110,000, and a kid pitcher named Billy Joe Davidson gets $100,000 and you know what I got out of the deal when it was all over? A cardboard suitcase.[11]

Also published in 1974, *Bad Henry* makes a brief but disdainful mention of the sale of Aaron's contract: "Henry was sold almost as a slave by the Clowns to the Braves." The hard tone of this statement was then softened somewhat with a follow-up quote from Aaron: "But," he says, "I'd have given $10,000 myself, had I known what it would be like in the majors."[12]

Almost twenty years later, in his autobiography with Lonnie Wheeler *I Had a Hammer*, the resentment over the deal seems to have dissipated, if not disappeared: "Mr. Pollock would have made more money in the long run if I had signed with the Giants, but there was no bonus money for me either way."[13]

Aaron's bonus came in the form of the aforementioned cardboard suitcase, a parting gift from Pollock that Aaron has recalled both fondly and spitefully in numerous accounts of this memorable time in his life. "I keep mentioning that cardboard suitcase . . . after I signed, Syd Pollock gave it to me for a going-away gift and in undying appreciation of the $10,000 I was putting in his pocket."[14]

In his book *When the Ball Had Life*, Syd Pollock's son, Alan Pollock, presents a more sympathetic version of his father's role in Aaron's signing with the Braves. As the younger Pollock recounts the story, Syd Pollock appealed in a letter to both Aaron and his parents to sign with the Braves for numerous reasons. Pollock had a longstanding relationship with the Boston club and believed he could exert some influence regarding issues such as where Henry might help the team and hopefully get him some playing time. Pollock stressed the fact that the Braves might have a greater need for a shortstop or second basemen than the

Giants and that they were willing to pay Henry $100 more per month than the Giants.

Before actually signing the Braves contract, Aaron's father, who would have to sign it for him because Henry was still a minor, brought it to a lawyer in Mobile to give it a professional reading. In the meantime, Aaron continued to play for the Clowns until his June 11 reporting date in Eau Claire. His final batting statistics with the Clowns have been grossly exaggerated and distorted in numerous historical references. Aaron has often been cited as having hit .467 during his brief stint with the Clowns, which may have been a batting average posted at some point early in the season or may have included his record in non-league exhibition games. However, the Howe Sports Bureau, which was responsible for recording the Negro American League statistics and disseminating them to media agencies, listed Aaron as having hit .366 in 26 official league games for Indianapolis with 5 home runs, 33 RBIs, 41 hits, and 9 stolen bases. Without exaggeration, Aaron played himself out of the league in a hurry. He signed his deal with the Boston Braves less than two weeks after his two big blasts on Opening Day in Baltimore. At the time of his departure, his batting average was tops among everyday players in the league and his other offensive totals were among the highest in the league as well.

As the rest of the 1952 Negro American League season played itself out, it was evident that the glory days of the Negro Leagues were gone. By the time Aaron had been picked to join the Indianapolis Clowns, Jackie Robinson's big league breakthrough and the subsequent departure of other star players had already begun to spell the demise of the Negro Leagues. It would all be over soon enough. It was fortunate for young Henry that the Negro Leagues still existed as an avenue to the big leagues when he was ready to break in.

NOTES

1. Aaron, with Wheeler, *I Had a Hammer*, 25.
2. Musick, *Hank Aaron*, 40.
3. Ibid., 41.
4. Henry Aaron, with Furman Bisher, *Aaron*, 2nd ed. (New York: Thomas E. Crowell Company, 1974), 18.
5. "Clowns Test Stares at Stadium Sunday," *Baltimore Afro-American,* May 17, 1952.
6. Aaron, with Wheeler, *I Had a Hammer*, 34.
7. Musick, *Hank Aaron*, 42.
8. Aaron, with Wheeler, *I Had a Hammer*, 36.
9. Ibid., 37.

10. Stan Baldwin and Jerry Jenkins, *Bad Henry* (Radnor, PA: Chilton Book Company, 1974), 138.

11. Aaron, with Bisher, *Aaron*, 19.

12. Baldwin and Jenkins, *Bad Henry*, 57.

13. Aaron, with Wheeler, *I Had a Hammer*, 38.

14. Aaron, with Bisher, *Aaron*, 20.

"EAU" TO BE YOUNG AGAIN—
EAU CLAIRE, WISCONSIN, 1952

The year 1952 is among the most pivotal years of Aaron's life. On June 8, just hours after the Indianapolis Clowns completed a double-header at Chicago's Comiskey Park, Henry Aaron, his brand new cardboard suitcase in hand, took the train to Milwaukee and then boarded an aircraft for the first time. Bound for Eau Claire, Wisconsin, where he would meet up with his teammates a few weeks shy of the midway point in the Northern League's season, he was scared half to death on what he described as the first and worst flight of his life.

Eau Claire was in northwestern Wisconsin 300 miles from Chicago, 1,200 miles from Mobile, Alabama, and so far removed from the world Aaron had lived in that it might as well have been an alien nation. For the first time in his life, Aaron would be playing baseball in an almost completely white town on an almost completely white team. Thankfully for Henry, there were two other black players on the Eau Claire Bears' roster, whom he lived with at the local YMCA. Outfielder Wes Covington, like Aaron, was a young, hopeful big-league prospect who the Braves held in high esteem. Catcher Julie Bowers was a prototypical career minor-leaguer, able to hold a spot on the team's roster but not quite good enough to harbor hopes of making it to the majors. Part coach, part mentor, part guardian, Bowers, according to Aaron, was the kind of black player found on many minor league teams of the time; his role was to keep company with and counsel younger black players on their way up. Aaron, Covington, and Bowers represented the second wave of black players to pass through Eau Claire for the Braves. Two years earlier, outfielders Bill Bruton, Horace Garner, and pitcher Roy White were the Braves first black trailblazers in the Northern

League. Bruton was the team's most valuable player and captured the league's Rookie of the Year Award. In 1953, he would become the first black player to play for the Braves in the majors. In Aaron's estimation, Bruton was possibly the most popular player in Eau Claire during Henry's season with the club, which began with warnings being issued to girls and women not be seen walking the town's streets with him. But Aaron and Covington would have had an even more difficult time being accepted and succeeding if Bruton had not first carved a path.

The Eau Claire community was not necessarily a hostile environment for black ballplayers; its citizens welcomed Aaron, Covington, and Bowers on the baseball field but they were not sure what to make of them around town. It was not unusual for Aaron to receive long hard stares while going about the ordinary business of his everyday life in a small Wisconsin town where many of the people had never seen a black person before. Aaron recalled incidents where young children would approach him and rub his skin to see if the black would come off. It took a while for the white people in Eau Claire to get accustomed to being around Henry, and he had little prior experience being around whites. Already a quiet person, being in Eau Claire made it even easier for Henry to keep to himself. Most of his conversations were with Covington, Bowers, and one white family that took him in as a kind of surrogate son, as often happens between minor league ballplayers and local baseball fans.

Henry developed a close friendship if not quite a romance with the family's teenage daughter; the pair kept their friendship private from the rest of the town. Overall, Aaron seems to have come away from Eau Claire with a generally favorable impression. In Phil Musick's biography of him, Aaron is quoted as saying that "It was very good, very good at Eau Claire. I didn't experience anything out of the way there, any racial trouble at all. I had a lot of white friends. People invited me to their homes for dinner."[1] However, years later in *I Had a Hammer*, Aaron did remember at least one near incident involving his relationship with the young white girl he had befriended: "Once she and I and Wes and Julie and a bunch of girls went up to a big hangout called Elks Mound, out in the country, and somehow a bunch of local guys found out and came looking for us. I don't know what they would have done if they had found us, but I wasn't eager to find out. The girls hid us in the bushes until they were gone."[2]

While Aaron wanted to get along with the white people of Eau Claire, it was of much less concern to him than playing ball against the white players of the Northern League. He was never short on confidence in his own abilities but throughout his brief life and time as a ballplayer in segregated leagues he had been fed a myth of white superiority that made him wonder if there was something different about how whites played baseball. It didn't take long to dispel such notions. In his first at-bat of his first game he had no trouble picking up a white ball thrown out of a white hand and smacked his first line drive single in "organized baseball." "When I came up in the second inning for my first time at bat in organized baseball," recalled Aaron in his memoir, "I was more nervous that it was my first time at bat against a white pitcher."[3]

"Organized baseball" is an expression coined by the major league baseball entity and its minor leagues in reference to itself. The term is defined in the *Dickson Baseball Dictionary* as "Professional baseball—that is, the Major and Minor Leagues as well as the offices that administer them."[4] Contained within the expression and its definition is a theft of the word "organized," as if the word itself and its meaning are somehow the property of major league baseball franchise owners and an underlying innuendo that any and all other forms of baseball are not organized.

While the Indianapolis Clowns' schedule may have been loosely organized within the Negro American League, including exhibition games against non-league teams, the baseball played by the Clowns and their opponents was still organized (since the team had a schedule and standing teams competed for a championship). It had obviously prepared Aaron well for the competition he would face in major league ball.

Aaron's debut did not escape the notice of the *Eau Claire Leader* newspaper, which reported the next day that "Hank Aaron, 18-year-old Negro League shortstop, made an auspicious beginning by banging out singles in his first two trips."[5] This may well have been the first time Aaron was referred to as "Hank" and not "Henry." Aaron himself later thought that the use of "Hank" began a couple of years later when he joined the Braves big league club in Milwaukee.

The first few weeks of the season were hard on Aaron: he experienced a new form of loneliness shared only by the select few black players accompanying him as teammates and opponents. Almost every aspect of life was different for a young black ballplayer so far from home. His speech patterns, the words he used and the way he spoke them immediately marked him as an outsider, and to gain entry and acceptance in this new world he practically had to learn a new language. He missed familiar things like his mother's cooking and the company of his friends and family. Almost overwhelmed by depression, he seriously considered packing it in, packing up his cardboard suitcase and heading back home. While he was still playing well enough to impress his teammates, manager, and scouts, a few on-field incidents contributed to his miserable feelings. While turning a double play against a team from Superior, Aaron's relay throw delivered in his criticized hip-shot style drilled the oncoming base runner right between the eyes. The player, a catcher named Chuck Wiles, was knocked unconscious, removed from the field on a stretcher and to Aaron's knowledge never played again. During the same week, Aaron was trying his hand at switch hitting in a batting practice session, lost his grip on the bat, and shattered a teammate's nose. He was so upset by the accident that he abandoned the idea of batting from the left-side ever again—which he later regretted—thinking that all the time he batted cross-handed might have made him a natural switch hitter. He called home and told his parents he was coming back, but his brother Herbert Jr. grabbed the phone and urged him to stick it out, explaining there was nothing in the way of opportunity waiting for him in Mobile. Sometime shortly thereafter, Henry knocked his first home run of the season for the Bears, a tenth-inning game winning blast that lifted his spirits and got him back on track.

A few weeks later Aaron had the highest batting average in the Northern League, and was voted the starting shortstop in the league's All Star Game, drawing the attention of former big league manager, Billy Southworth, one of the Braves foremost scouts. "For a baby-face kid of 18 years his playing ability is outstanding," wrote Southworth in his initial report on Aaron.[6]

Aaron also found an ally in manager Bill Adair. Like Aaron, Adair was from Alabama, which, depending the autobiography, Aaron saw as either a good or bad thing. In his 1974 *Aaron* autobiography with Furman Bisher, Aaron writes: "A guy couldn't have asked to break in under a better manager than Bill Adair. He was from Montgomery, Alabama, and I think because he was a Southerner he was even a little more understanding of the little black kid he had playing beside him."[7] Almost 20 years later, the same situation is recalled in stark contrast to the previous account, in Aaron's *I Had a Hammer*, coauthored with Lonnie Wheeler and published in 1991: "The first thing I found out about Adair was that he was from Mobile, which I didn't receive as thrilling news. I knew how white people from Mobile thought about black people from Mobile, and I wondered if I could ever be the equal of a white player in his eyes."[8]

The opposing viewpoints contained in at least these two authorized autobiographies may have been influenced by the coauthors, their relative backgrounds, subjective interpretations, and opinions. Bisher was a beat reporter for an Atlanta newspaper, who covered Aaron during the trying and tumultuous era of his closing in on Babe Ruth's record. There seems to be a conscious effort being made throughout the Bisher book to skirt away from controversial opinions or judgmental statements. The fourth chapter of the book that deals with the time Aaron spent breaking the South Atlantic League color line in Jacksonville, Florida, begins with a statement by Aaron that almost reads as a disclaimer for the delicate account to follow: "I'm no crusader, not in the way they use the word now. Never wanted to be. Let's get that straight before we go any further."[9]

In the introduction to Wheeler's book, these discrepancies in the historical record are addressed as follows:

> We had the same book in mind . . . and his recollections were persuasively reinforced by the most reliable of sources. This was not a point to be taken for granted, because the popular versions of Aaron's past were not always consistent with the facts. The media for instance, commonly advanced the notion that Aaron never spoke out about civil rights. . . . But Aaron maintained that he had stepped forward on racial issues throughout his career, and the old articles bear him out.[10]

By the time *Home Run: My Life in Pictures* was written with Dick Schaap and published in 1999, Aaron and his coauthors were quite comfortable in dealing with Aaron's opinions on race: "I love being who I am. I love what I've accomplished and I still look forward to accomplishing more, to continuing my campaigns to give African-Americans equal opportunities in baseball and outside of baseball. (As a man who remembers clearly when African-Americans were not welcome in Organized Baseball, I know how far we've come.)"[11]

Returning to the subject of manager Bill Adair, despite how his being from Alabama may have been initially interpreted by Aaron, in the end just about every historical account of their time together concludes with the opinion that Adair's treatment and assessment of Aaron was even-handed.

Adair, who doubled as the team's second baseman playing next to Aaron in the infield, shared the consensus opinion on Aaron's fielding abilities reported by the scouts and was not sure how to interpret Aaron's ultra-calm demeanor and aloof personality. "Nobody can guess his IQ," Adair wrote in an early progress report, "because he gives you nothing to go on." However, Adair was won over by Aaron's consistency at the plate. "He may not be a major-league shortstop, but as a hitter he has everything."[12] As the season wore on, Aaron believed Adair was more than fair in his treatment of him as player and the two developed a mutual respect for each other.

By season's end, Aaron batted .336 with 9 home runs, 61 RBIs, and 116 hits in 87 games and was named the Northern League's Rookie of the Year. Referring to him by two first names, the *Eau Claire Leader* summed up Aaron's season as follows:

> Henry (Hank) Aaron the 18-year-old Mobile, Ala., colored shortstop for the Eau Claire Bears, has been named as the outstanding rookie in the Northern League for the 1952 season. In a poll of sports writers, managers and umpires, Aaron rolled up 75 points. . . . Other

players who got votes for first place included John Covington, Eau
Claire colored outfielder and John Goryl, Eau Claire third base-
man. . . . Aaron is the third of his race to win the George Treadwell—
Duluth Dukes Memorial Award.[13]

In the newspaper's account, both Aaron and Covington are identified first by
color and then by position. Five years after Jackie Robinson's major league breakthrough, about two dozen African Americans had integrated the big leagues, with
dozens more toiling for minor league affiliates, but apparently the presence of
these players was not enough for them to be identified without racial modifiers.

Aaron was the third consecutive Eau Claire player to win the league's Rookie
of the Year award, following Bill Bruton and Horace Garner, but Aaron noticed
that this was less significant to the newspaper than the fact that he was black.
The identification of players by color was a practice that would continue for
many more years.

At this time, Aaron began to recognize the patterns by which certain black
players were treated. At the same time, he realized that as a top prospect he was
receiving special treatment and being looked after both on and off the field.
Aaron credited Braves general manager John Mullen with keeping him out of
trouble by insisting Aaron register with the draft board during the Korean War.

Aaron escaped the fate of being drafted during the war, but his teammate
Covington was not as lucky. The two had shared their hopes and dreams during the splendid season they spent in the Northern League and had imagined
making it to the majors together some day. When Covington was drafted in
1953, his dreams were put on hold and the best he could do was live vicariously
through Aaron until he made it back. "I told Hank I was going to have to go
fight the war for him, but when I got out I would just do things right behind
him—whatever he did, I'd come along and do the same thing. Well, the next
year he won the batting title at Jacksonville, and the first year I was back, I won
the batting title at Jacksonville," recalled Covington.[14] The pair would not play
together again until Covington joined Aaron with the Braves in 1956.

When the 1952 Northern League season came to a close, Aaron hooked up
with his Indianapolis Clowns team from the beginning of the same season just
in time to participate in the Negro League World Series against the Birmingham Black Barons. Aaron joined his old mates, or what was left of them, at the
start of a best-of-thirteen-games barnstorming-style series that would be played
all over the South.

Although he was still considerably younger than most of the other Clowns,
Aaron returned a few months after his departure with an almost veteran presence. He hadn't been all the way to the big leagues yet, but he had been to a

world the rest of them had never and probably would never see or know. Picking up right where he left off, Aaron hit .402 with 5 home runs in the Clowns seven-games-to-5 victory over Birmingham.

Aaron viewed his reassignment with the club as off-season employment and a means of making a little extra money before heading back home to Mobile for the winter. The series started in Memphis, continuing in Little Rock and Hot Springs Arkansas; Nashville; and Welch, West Virginia, in the Blue Ridge Mountains, a regular Negro league barnstorming stop where Aaron hit a memorable series blast that drew even more references to Josh Gibson. From Welch, the series moved on to Bluefield, West Virginia; Newport News and Norfolk, Virginia; and Columbus, Georgia. The tenth game of the series was Aaron's first homecoming visit to Mobile since leaving town for spring training; a local black organization called the Dragon Social Club proclaimed it Henry Aaron Day at Hartwell Field, which was a surreal experience for Henry, who had never played there before. Hartwell Field was predominantly used as the home field for the white Southern League's Mobile Bears, or for major league exhibition games. Most of the time a specific portion of the stadium was designated for black fans, but on this day the process was reversed and the grandstand served as the seating area for white fans. The Clowns, who had been trailing five games to four, won that day to even up the series and then traveled to Biloxi, Mississippi, and New Orleans, winning in both cities to capture the championship in one of the last official Negro League World Series.

NOTES

1. Musick, *Hank Aaron*, 46.
2. Aaron, with Wheeler, *I Had a Hammer*, 41.
3. Ibid., 42.
4. Paul Dickson, *The Baseball Dictionary* (New York: Facts on File, 1989), 286.
5. Aaron, with Wheeler, *I Had a Hammer*, 42.
6. Baldwin and Jenkins, *Bad Henry*, 284.
7. Aaron, with Bisher, *Aaron*, 22.
8. Aaron, with Wheeler, *I Had a Hammer*, 44.
9. Aaron, with Bisher, *Aaron*, 27.
10. Aaron, with Wheeler, *I Had a Hammer*, xi.
11. Henry Aaron, with Dick Schaap, *Home Run: My Life in Pictures* (Kingston, NY: Total Sports, 1999), 21.
12. Aaron, with Wheeler, *I Had a Hammer*, 44.
13. Ibid., 46.
14. Ibid., 47.

INTEGRATING BASEBALL IN THE DEEP SOUTH— JACKSONVILLE, FLORIDA, 1953

Henry Aaron was still a teenager when he reported to the Braves spring training camp in Kissimmee, Florida, shortly after celebrating his 19th birthday in February 1953. But there is something about being away from home, living on the road, and working under extreme pressure and constant scrutiny that has a way of turning a child into a man. Aaron was not the same scared kid boarding a train to unknown frontiers that he was a year before. So much had happened since then it seemed as if that day belonged to another life, to someone else's life. Although Aaron was still a skinny kid, he already had one monumental year behind him, limitless possibility in front of him, and the upcoming season presented even more opportunity for growth. Despite whatever flaws in his fielding Billy Southworth may have reported to the Braves organization, Aaron's undeniable ability with a bat left such a favorable impression upon all concerned that it seemed inevitable that he would climb to the next level ahead of schedule. In workman like fashion, Aaron, humbly if not quite unconsciously, continued to realize the potential everyone saw in him.

At the start of spring training Aaron was initially assigned to the AAA Milwaukee Brewers, the Braves highest-level farm club, which was a big leap from Class-C Eau Claire. However, Aaron had earned the invitation by merit of his stellar performance during the previous season. While it was flattering to be included on the AAA roster, it soon became apparent that it was little more than a gesture; Aaron received little playing time during the first few weeks. Aaron himself cited a combination of reasons keeping him off the field. Most of the time he was either the only black player or one of two on the Brewer's spring roster and on at least one occasion this was reason enough for him to be banned from playing.

After traveling with the team to Winter Haven, Florida, for an exhibition game with the Boston Red Sox, Aaron was not allowed to play because of segregation. He was told by some form of local authority not to get off the team bus, thus he was not able to show off his talents to the Braves. Back on the home turf in Kissimmee, Brewers manager Tommy Holmes, an accomplished and knowledgeable batsman in his time, was critical of Aaron's unorthodox approach to hitting. In his recently completed 11-year career (10 with the Braves), Holmes was a lifetime .302 hitter, including a whopping .352 in 1945 when he also set a National League standard by hitting in 37 consecutive games. Holmes served as an interim manager for the Braves from the end of the 1951 season through the beginning of the 1952 campaign. He figured that he knew a thing or two about hitting and saw passing that information on and correcting his players' flaws as a primary responsibility in his capacity as a minor league manager. He was particularly put off by Aaron's opposite field hitting and almost immediately dismissed him as a serious major league prospect. Holmes told Braves farm director John Mullen that unless Aaron learned to pull the ball he would never make it in the big leagues, and Holmes didn't think the Triple-A level was the right place to receive the type of instruction and experience to make the necessary adjustments.

On the rare occasion that Holmes penciled Aaron's name onto the line-up card that spring, Aaron claims to have hit the ball well and with power, knocking at least one home run to right field, which was the wrong field as far as Holmes was concerned. Aaron assumed he would never be included on the Brewers regular-season roster and midway through spring training he asked Mullen if he could be reassigned at a lower level where he might have more of an opportunity to play. Mullen placed Aaron on the Class A Jacksonville club that trained in Waycross, Georgia. At about this same time, on March 18, the Boston Braves announced that the major league franchise would be moving to Milwaukee. General manager John Quinn visited the big league camp in Brandenton and passed out new caps with an "M" on them where the "B" used to be. The Triple-A Milwaukee Brewers organization would move its operation to Toledo, Ohio, where Aaron would never play.

At Waycross, Aaron was immediately inserted as an everyday player and throughout the remainder of the spring kept smacking the wood on horsehide with a thunderous crack that caught the attention of anyone within earshot. The move down came as a blessing in disguise for Aaron. Paired in the Jacksonville infield with Felix Mantilla, the best shortstop in the Braves organization, Aaron was given the opportunity to learn a new position as he was moved over to second; the two top prospects created a formidable nucleus of what would become a solid team. The Jacksonville Tars squad was captained by a hard-nosed, hard-drinking but sensitive and compassionate baseball man named Ben Geraghty.

Aaron has credited Geraghty with instilling in him an essential component of his development as a player by teaching him to be a student of the game. In every written account of Aaron's career, he has reiterated that Geraghty was the most influential manager he played for. "He was the greatest manager I ever played for, perhaps the greatest manager who ever lived, and that includes managers in the big leagues. I've never played for a guy who could get more out of every ballplayer than he could. He knew how to communicate with everybody and to treat every player as an individual."[1]

Playing for Jacksonville also presented Aaron with the newest and biggest challenge of his professional career, a task of Jackie Robinson-sized proportions. Along with teammates Mantilla and outfielder Horace Garner as well as two Savannah players, Junior Reedy and Al Isreal, the group of five became the first black players in the fifty-year history of the South Atlantic League (known as the Sally League). It fell upon Geraghty to help Aaron navigate his way through the turbulence that would undoubtedly follow. Jacksonville would also be the introduction to a running theme in Aaron's life that would have him at the center of dramatic transitional periods in American history unfolding on a national stage.

Aaron and the four others' assignments put them in the eye of a storm that had been picking up momentum since Robinson's breakthrough. While almost all the major league teams had been integrated by the opening of the 1952 season, the minor leagues of the Deep South had stood in open opposition to the new policy of their major league affiliates. But the tide was turning, and time and circumstance were not on the side of the segregationists in baseball or elsewhere in American society. Neither were many of the white teammates and coaches of black players throughout the minor leagues. Author Bruce Adelson chronicled the desegregation of minor league baseball in the American South in his book, *Brushing Back Jim Crow*. In recounting the events of 1952, Adelson cited an incident of April 2 in Bartow, Florida, in which a local city ordinance barred black players from the clubhouse of Municipal Stadium where the Braves Triple-A Milwaukee Brewers were scheduled to play an exhibition game with the Buffalo Bisons. When Brewers players were informed that their teammate Jim "Buster" Clarkson would not be allowed access to the clubhouse and would have to dress at the National Guard Armory across the street, they spoke up: "We dress where he (Jim) dresses," and went with Clarkson to the armory.[2]

By the time Aaron broke in, baseball's integration movement was successfully and progressively moving towards an era when African Americans would be among the game's most dominant players. Larry Doby became the American League's first black player six weeks after Robinson broke through. Pitcher Dan Bankhead joined the Dodgers late in the 1947 season, and Hank Thompson and Willard Brown became St. Louis Browns before the end of the campaign. Although it was late in his career, pitcher Satchel Paige, already a legend from his days in the Negro Leagues, joined Doby on the Indians in 1948 while catcher Roy Campanella became Robinson's teammate in Brooklyn. Luke Easter (Cleveland), Monte Irvin (New York Giants), Minnie Minoso (Cleveland), and Don Newcombe (Brooklyn) were the class of 1949. Sam Jethroe, not Aaron, was the first black player signed by the Braves when the team was still in Boston in 1950. Willie Mays arrived with the Giants and won the Rookie of the Year Award in 1951.

These players' performances enlightened baseball fans and baseball's business community and won over many converts who had to see what black players were capable of doing before accepting that African Americans were able to play alongside white major leaguers. It took a few years for this sentiment to be shared by baseball fans in the Deep South. "Negroes in baseball was sure to come South. It has been a gradual movement, but one that was inevitable. And I personally say: What's the difference if the boy is a good ballplayer. Anyway, there's nobody that can stop it," said a fan at Opening Day in Savannah on April 14, 1953.[3]

The arrival of Aaron and others in the South Atlantic League was reluctantly accepted by a portion of white fans in the Deep South. However, it came much to the delight of southern black baseball fans who had eagerly anticipated this day since the integration of major league baseball in 1947. The effect of having black players on two of the South Atlantic League's rosters paid immediate dividends at the turnstiles. More than 5,000 fans, the largest number for any league's 1953 Opening Day, and the South Atlantic League's biggest crowd of the year, were on hand when Jacksonville came to Savannah to start the season by defeating the Indians 6–4. It was a sign of things to come for a talent-laden Jacksonville squad led by its black players—Garner, Mantilla, and most notably Aaron.

Approximately half of the crowd on Opening Day were African Americans, who, the *Savannah Morning News* reported, "completely filled one section of the left field bleachers."[4] The addition of African American fans attending games at South Atlantic League ballparks created one of the most significant hikes in attendance from one year to the next in league history. In Jacksonville alone, the average number of black fans attending games doubled, and the team's season attendance total of 142,721 was more than twice the total for 1952.

Increased attendance was enjoyed by the league's other clubs—in cities like

Columbia and Charleston, South Carolina; Macon, Alabama; and Columbus, Augusta, and Savannah, Georgia—whenever Jacksonville was in town. The enthusiastic fan response to Aaron and his Jacksonville mates caused seats to be added in just about every Sally League ballpark, and led team owners to reconsider their stance on segregation.

The burgeoning crowds created a diverse cultural dichotomy at ballparks around the league. The handful of black players and the idea of integrated baseball in the South were met with widely varying reactions from black and white fans, players, and baseball hierarchy. In most of the Sally League ballparks, fan seating was segregated, with black fans usually relegated to bleacher seats on one side of the outfield. In Jacksonville, that area was left field, where the fans' response to Aaron, Garner, and Mantilla was wildly enthusiastic.

It was the same on the road, where the significance of history in the making was not lost on black fans who came out in droves to catch a glimpse of Aaron and the others. Aaron's own recollections of this period contain a broad spectrum of emotions, and the historical record again presents conflicting interpretations. The wide disparity in his opinions and remembrances of this eventful time in his life could be due in part to the fact that so many good and bad things were happening to him at the same time. As Aaron recalled:

> We set all kinds of records that year and opened up the Sally League to a whole new group of customers. There were so many black fans that they had to add room to the colored section in a lot of the ballparks. Columbia had a rickety old ballpark and one night the colored section got so full, and the people got to rocking it so hard, that it collapsed. It was like a party every night in the colored section. All we had to do was catch a fly ball and every body would whoop and holler like we won the World Series.[5]

In Phil Musick's 1974 biography, Aaron recalled the cool initial reception he received from white fans at parks in cities like Montgomery, Savannah, and Asheville. "For more than a month, white people wouldn't applaud us, but finally we won them over."[6] Nonetheless, amidst the excitement stirred by events taking place on the field, tension and animosity developed among white and black fans; vitriolic verbal exchanges were launched back and forth between the white and black sections of the ballparks.

The "great experiment," a term coined to describe the Jackie Robinson experience, was taking place not only on the country's baseball diamonds but in the seats as well. Aaron and the others had brought the great experiment to a partially hostile and unwelcome environment. With baseball as the common denominator, the presence of Aaron and other black players created a previously unseen comingling of the races. There was probably nowhere else in the south where so many white and black people could be found in the same place. As Aaron recalled, "Horace and Felix and I knew that we had to shut out everything else and play ball, but when we looked up at all those black and white faces screaming at us, we couldn't help but feel the weight of what we were doing."[7]

Certain aspects of the season and playing in the south are recalled fondly by Aaron in a cautious way of dealing with the past. In another apologetic disclaimer for the racially charged recounting of his time spent in the Sally League, this time for his 1974 autobiography written with Furman Bisher, Aaron says, "I ought to point out here that just getting to the major leagues didn't eliminate segregation. You know, I don't like that word. Every time I use it, it makes me feel like I'm complaining. I feel like I'm charging somebody with a crime. I don't feel that way at all. This country has been good to me and I've had a great life."[8]

In the same chapter, a heated confrontation between shortstop Mantilla and a Macon pitcher named John Waselchuk—resulting in a near riot between white and back fans—is glossed over.

> There were only two "incidents" that disturbed the scene on a racial basis that season, and I'm not even sure one was based on race. It took place in Macon. The Macon team had an old pitcher, a tough-looking guy who always looked like he needed a shave. Felix was mighty young looking then, had almost a baby face. When he would come to bat, this pitcher would growl at him.
>
> "Pickaninny, ain't you too young to be away from yo' mammy?" Stuff like that. Not loud. Not long. Just a thing or two to try and scare him so he wouldn't play his best. . . . One night in Macon this old pitcher was pitching Felix pretty "tight." One of the pitches hit him, and by this time Felix was boiling. Felix charged the mound, and the Macon players charged Felix, and the Jacksonville players charged the Macon players. About this time, a couple of hot headed fans jumped out of the stands and ran out on the field. Police moved in and more police came out on an emergency call, it said in the paper the next day, but it was all broken up before anybody got hurt.[9]

These types of barnyard brawls were nothing new to baseball even when the game was segregated, but the use of the word "pickaninny" would have to be considered racially charged and it seems uncharacteristic of Aaron, especially the outspoken Aaron of later years, to let it escape scrutiny.

The same story is given much more serious treatment in the book Aaron wrote with Lonnie Wheeler in 1991.

> Meanwhile the people from the white section along first base were coming over the railing and people from the colored section were headed over to the white section. It was real close to being a race riot. They called the police and after order was restored, the policemen ringed the field and stood there with their hands on their guns.[10]

The mention of only "two incidents" in the Bisher book also appears to be a gross understatement in light of the attitudes and conditions revealed to have existed throughout the league at the time. Just a few pages earlier in the book, the entire period Aaron spent in the Sally League and the unequal treatment he received there is off-handedly dismissed.

> It must have been bad, the way black players were handled, but I'd never been anywhere before; I'd been raised in the south, and this was the way I was accustomed to seeing blacks treated. So I knew what to expect, and I think Garner did too. Mantilla was just two years way from Puerto Rico, though, and it was puzzling to him.
>
> Besides, I was having such a good year and I was so loose that I must have been a barrel of fun. At least, that's what I read in the newspapers from time to time.[11]

The light treatment given by Aaron and Bisher to this tumultuous time is in direct contrast with other descriptive accounts given by Aaron at both the same time and in more recent years. In Bruce Adelson's *Brushing Back Jim Crow*, Aaron is quoted as saying the following:

> I couldn't put my finger on which city in the league was the worst for me to play in. I would say all of them. In fact, at the beginning, even Jacksonville could be included. Columbus was as bad as Jacksonville. Jacksonville was as bad as Montgomery was. They all had their problems. They just weren't used to black and white players playing together.[12]

In Phil Musick's 1974 book, *Hank Aaron: The Man Who Beat the Babe*, Aaron is quoted as saying:

> Playing in the Sally league was a very bad experience for me. "Jigaboo . . . burr-head." They called me names I never heard of before.

Or maybe I'd heard them and they went in one ear and out the other. Maybe I was too dumb as a kid to get mad. I'm not hot tempered. I wouldn't think about what was said to me from the stands. If I'd gotten those kinds of names on the street, it might've been different.[13]

While playing in the Sally League may have been an emotionally trying experience for Aaron, it was also one of the most productive times for him as a player. His focused determination enabled him to channel feelings like anger, fear, and frustration into his playing.

On one particularly hot summer night in Augusta, Georgia, yet another riotous group of fans hurled rocks along with the usual racial epithets at Aaron's teammate Horace Garner as he played his position in the outfield. An umpire used the public address system to insist that the fans refrain from their disorderly conduct. The group became even more hostile and escalated their racist catcalls to the point of threatening violent—even homicidal—behavior. Aaron remembered them saying, "Nigger, we're gonna kill you next time. Ain't no nigger gonna squawk on no white folks down here."[14]

Aaron, Garner, and Mantilla's response took the form of 13 hits in 14 collective at-bats, which would be Aaron's continual answer to the racist baiting he received throughout the 1953 season. In fact, when manager Geraghty informed Aaron that he and the others would be the first black players this part of the Deep South had ever seen, Aaron accepted his situation as just another challenge. His personal way of dealing with it would be to "play so good they can't remember what color you were before the season started."[15]

On the road, the team traveled by bus and while the bus was in motion Aaron was still included. He could talk baseball with his teammates and coaches. He could laugh and play card games to while away the time, but when the bus stopped for meals and their white teammates stepped off to enter a restaurant, Aaron, Garner, and Mantilla remained on the bus. At times like these, any sense of inclusion Aaron might have felt would slip away and his entire world was only as big as the inside of that bus. Somebody would bring some food back and Aaron, Garner, and Mantilla would eat their meals in their separate space. While the rest of the players might use the restroom before boarding the bus, the three black players would have to wait until the bus was rolling again and a suitable place to park could be found on the side of the road along the way. Back on the bus, life would resume as if nothing unusual had happened and the fun and frolicking would continue until the team reached its hotel and the white players once again disembarked leaving Aaron, Garner, and Mantilla behind. As Aaron recalled, "We'd come into town laughing and joking, but when the unloading started at the hotel everything got quiet."[16]

Like Jackie Robinson before him, he was told that for him to continue to play and succeed he would have to do so quietly. Even in the face of open hostility, racial discrimination, and obvious injustice, retaliation was not an option. On Opening Day, the umpiring crew working the game between Jacksonville and Savannah addressed all five of the league's new black players, laying down the law. Arguing any calls was strictly forbidden, which, provided that calls were made in earnest, seemed fair enough, but they were also told not to strike back even when struck. Should they be spiked, pushed, punched, or beaned by a ball, there would be no fighting back. So Aaron and the others made the best of it and tried to go about their business on the field and, with only a few incidental exceptions like Mantilla's moment in Macon, they did just that. Like Bill Bruton and Horace Garner had done before them in Eau Claire, Aaron and his contemporaries were cutting a swath through the South, widening the path for others to follow. That's how Aaron looked back on his time in Jacksonville.

> The next year, [Jacksonville] had Juan Pizarro, the left-handed pitcher, and they kept on building on what we had done. If we had failed, if we had come to the South and started arguing, fighting, and not having a good year, there would have been something for the press to talk about. There would have been something for the league to talk about. It would certainly have been something for everyone to say, "I told you so." By the Braves sending us here to play baseball—and I had probably one of the best years I ever had in baseball, and Horace and Felix both had good years, and Felix and I got to the major leagues off this team—we proved that by just being given the opportunity, we could play baseball.[17]

From a baseball standpoint, the south was desirable for a number of reasons; it was the traditional domain of minor league baseball, with warm, inviting weather perfectly conducive for young prospects to get a feel for the game. But the Sally League's and the other southern leagues' long standing legacy of segregation led them to stubbornly retain that legacy even when they were asked to accept blacks by such major league baseball mavericks as Branch Rickey and Bill Veeck. It would be left to young black players like Aaron to fight this battle on the front lines. As Aaron later explained, "I wasn't prepared for what would happen that year. When I played in Jacksonville, there were things that happened to me that happened to Jackie Robinson before and after he got to the big leagues. Baseball was having problems in Georgia, in the South and all over."[18]

As recently as 1952, black players were still being banned from teams in southern leagues. Jacksonville itself had shut its ballpark down, citing a city ordinance, rather than let Jackie Robinson and pitcher John Wright play in an exhibition game in 1947. The old Southern League fought integration to the bitter end, allowing a lone black player but one at-bat before eventually shutting down operations in 1961.

In 1953, the Tars tore out of the gates with a seven-game winning streak beginning on Opening Day and they pulled away from the rest of the Sally League by the All-Star break. Aaron never regretted not playing for Triple-A Toledo that year and despite Jacksonville's lower classification, the Tars may have had a better ball club. Working under intense pressure and difficult living conditions, Aaron, Garner, and Mantilla blocked out the fans' racist baiting and played well from the outset of the season. Aaron knew as early as spring training that Jacksonville would field a formidable team. First baseman Joe Andrews led the league in hitting for the first month and battled with Aaron for the league batting title throughout the season. Garner was a power hitter and possessed one of the strongest throwing arms that Aaron can remember seeing. Left fielder Jim Frey, a future big league manager, became a friend and ally of Aaron's and especially of Garner, with whom he shared outfield responsibilities that made him aware of the abuse heaped upon Garner by many fans along the Sally League circuit. Frey later recalled the following:

> The first situation I got was in Savannah. When we came out of the clubhouse, we had to walk through the stands, right past the fans. They were awful. They were lined up on both sides of us. Their remarks to the black players were absolutely horrible.
>
> By the time I got to Jacksonville, the seed had been planted, I guess. I was sympathetic to the black players I came in contact with. When I saw segregation firsthand and heard the daily verbal abuse, it was something I didn't like. It was hard on everybody. Multiply this many times for blacks and what they had to deal with.[19]

Joe Andrews, Jacksonville's resident tough guy and hell raiser, also took up the cause of his black teammates. Andrews was a hard-drinking, hard-living, curfew-breaking headache to manager Geraghty. But he watched over Aaron, Garner, and Mantilla like a big brother and served as their personal bodyguard, escorting them out of ballparks at night with a bat in his hand and instructing them to stay close by his side. Andrews spoke up on Aaron's behalf to fans, opponents, and teammates alike whenever he saw injustice being perpetrated. As Andrews later remembered,

> It wasn't just the fans, either. We had a few Southern boys on our ball club, and they'd say things. Henry came up with a couple of men on

base once when we were down by a run, and he popped up to end the game. Afterwards, somebody on our team said, "Well, when pull comes to tug, a nigger's gonna croak every time." I just started screaming. We didn't need to be worrying about our guys, because we had enough problems with the rednecks on the other side.[20]

Manager Geraghty was also constantly on Aaron's side and made a point of spending time with the black players wherever their separate accommodations would have them on the road. Whether it was a boarding house or blacks-only hotel, Geraghty would stop by in the evenings after games to knock back a few beers and talk baseball, his two favorite things. It made Aaron, Garner, and Mantilla feel appreciated as part of the team. Aaron recalled a night in Columbus when the team was invited to dinner at Fort Benning and the black players were told they were not allowed to eat in the dining room—Geraghty joined them for the meal in the kitchen.

At the time of the All-Star break, Aaron was leading the league in many offensive categories and was one of five Jacksonville players named to the All-Star team. The game was scheduled to be played in Savannah, where the governor of Georgia, Herman Talmadge, a hardline segregationist who had recently conducted a national campaign opposed to blacks and whites appearing together on television, had expressed the desire to keep Aaron from participating. It struck Aaron as rather odd considering he had been playing games in Savannah throughout the season. Aaron had every intention of playing in the All Star Game but it became a moot point the day before the game when he had his big toe nail ripped off in a run down play in the same Savannah ballpark. Aaron was already bothered by the fact that neither Garner nor Mantilla had been originally named to the team, and he became even more concerned when Felix, who was hitting .300 and Aaron's superior in the field, was not chosen to take his place when he was injured.

While segregationalists may have been able to keep black players off All-Star rosters, they could not eliminate their names from the league's statistical records. At the end of the season, Aaron's name was at the top of the list in batting average (.362), runs batted in (125), runs scored (115), base hits (208), and doubles (36). His 22 home runs were one behind the leader and his 14 triples also placed him second. His batting average was 20 points in front of his closest competitor, and no one else in the league reached even 100 RBIs. As one writer said, "Aaron led the league in everything except hotel accommodations."[21] He was a shoo-in for the league's MVP award, receiving 12 of 16 votes cast, and he was the only unanimous choice for the 12-man season's end All-Star team for which there was no exhibition game.

On October 25, 1953, a newspaper story titled "Braves Teen Age Hopefuls" by reporter Joe Livingston summed up the seasons of Aaron and Mantilla as follows:

> **Jacksonville, Fla.**—Two teen age ballplayers, each with only two years of professional experience behind him, are being cited by fans here as sure fire future regulars on the Milwaukee Braves. One is slugger Henry Aaron, age 19, from Mobile, Ala., presently a second baseman. The other is Felix Mantilla, 18, from Isabella, Puerto Rico, by trade a shortstop. The Braves will take a look at them both next spring training.

After discussing their skills and accomplishments the story assessed the personalities of both ballplayers.

> Of the two, Mantilla is more temperamental. Although the total was not excessive, he was more prone to dispute with umpires. Aaron, soft spoken when he speaks at all, followed closely the suggestion that Negro players in their first venture in the Deep South league should pay attention solely to application of their own talents to the game.[22]

Jacksonville advanced to the playoffs and defeated Savannah in its opening series but lost the league championship to Columbia. Naturally, Aaron and his mates were disappointed to have lost the playoffs, but a greater victory had already been won. The South Atlantic League's version of baseball's "Great Experiment" was completed and even South Atlantic president Dick Butler had declared it a success. Butler had been monitoring Aaron's progress all season long: "I traveled with Jacksonville because most of the focus was on Aaron. Aaron probably didn't know it, but all year long I followed Jacksonville and sat in the stands to sort of keep a lookout. You never knew what was going to happen. Those people had awfully strong feelings about what was going on."[23]

What was going on was the tearing down and rebuilding of a southern institution that had been segregated for fifty years. A *Jacksonville Journal* columnist placed the credit squarely on Aaron's shoulders: "I sincerely believe Aaron may have started Jacksonville down the road to racial understanding."[24] He may not have realized it at the time, but years later Aaron wondered if he had ever done anything more important.

NOTES

1. Cohen, *Hammerin' Hank of the Braves*, 32.

2. Bruce Adelson, *Brushing Back Jim Crow: The Integration of Minor-League Baseball in the American South* (Charlottesville: University Press of Virginia Press, 1999), 51.

3. Ibid., 83.

4. Ibid., 84.

5. Aaron, with Wheeler, *I Had a Hammer*, 57.

6. Musick, *Hank Aaron*, 51.

7. Aaron, with Wheeler, *I Had a Hammer*, 57.

8. Aaron, with Bisher, *Aaron*, 38.

9. Ibid., 36.

10. Aaron, with Wheeler, *I Had a Hammer*, 59.

11. Aaron, with Bisher, *Aaron*, 32.

12. Adelson, *Brushing Back Jim Crow*, 89.

13. Musick, *Hank Aaron*, 52.

14. Aaron, with Wheeler, *I Had a Hammer*, 59.

15. Aaron, with Bisher, *Aaron*, 31.

16. Musick, *Hank Aaron*, 51.

17. Adelson, *Brushing Back Jim Crow*, 88.

18. Ibid.

19. Ibid., 91.

20. Aaron, with Wheeler, *I Had a Hammer*, 61.

21. Aaron, with Bisher, *Aaron*, 32.

22. Joe Livingston, "Braves Teen Age Hopefuls," *Milwaukee Journal*, October 25, 1953.

23. Aaron, with Wheeler, *I Had a Hammer*, 58.

24. Ibid., 75.

Twenty-year-old rookie infielder Henry Aaron strikes a pose during Florida spring training in 1954. *National Baseball Hall of Fame Library, Cooperstown, N.Y.*

BROKEN BONES AND OTHER
BREAKS, 1953–1954

As much as he loved baseball and as busy as he was chasing down his dream during the 1953 season in Jacksonville, Aaron found time for at least one other pursuit. Her name was Barbara Lucas. Sometime around the beginning of the season, shortly after Aaron and his teammates had settled into their new living quarters near the ballpark in a house owned by a black man named Manuel who also operated a local saloon named "Manuel's," Aaron got his first glimpse of Barbara. Hanging around the ballpark one day, he spied a young woman he assumed was about his age, walking into the post office; he asked the team's clubhouse attendant who she might be. The clubbie was a local man named T. C. Marlin who knew everybody in town. He told Aaron that the girl in question was named Barbara Lucas, who was visiting her home after being away at Florida A&M University. She was also enrolled in classes at a local business college. Aaron had Marlin introduce him to Barbara as a future big league baseball star, which, as he recalled later, left her unimpressed. However, she agreed to go out on a date with him if he would first visit her home and meet her parents. The pair quickly became comfortable in each other's company and when the team was playing its home games in town Aaron spent much of his time at the Lucas home.

As is often the case for a young ballplayer, many young women approached Aaron while the team was on the road. Aaron admitted to having a romantic interest early in the 1953 season with a woman who lived in Phenix City across the Alabama border from where the team played in Columbus, Georgia. Phenix City was a wild town with open drinking and gambling on the streets at night and Aaron had to maneuver his way around these activities to get to and from the house of the woman he was seeing. It was probably not the safest place for a solitary young black man to be wandering around in the Deep South late in the evening. One particular night on his way back to where he was staying, he was chased through the streets and across the Chattahoochee River into Georgia. It is the last time Aaron remembered meeting up with that particular woman until she paid him a surprise visit in Jacksonville later in the season, by which time he had already committed himself to the idea of marrying Barbara. By the time the season was over, he let Barbara know his intentions. On the night of the team's end of season banquet, during which Aaron was honored with the Most Valuable Player award, he broke away from the festivities momentarily and telephoned Barbara from the banquet and asked her to marry him. Barbara's immediate response was for Hank to ask her father's permission. Mr. Lucas worked on the railroad as a Pullman porter, and at the time could not see a bright future for a young black man in professional baseball, but he must have believed in Aaron's sincerity. Mr. Lucas was the porter on the train that brought Barbara to Mobile to meet Aaron's family. The couple was married on October 13, 1953, and lived with Aaron's parents for a brief stint following their wedding.

During this time, Aaron was contacted by teammate Felix Mantilla who had also married a Jacksonville girl at the conclusion of the season. Mantilla was returning to his home in Puerto Rico to play winter league ball for a team in the country town of Caguas and asked Aaron if he and Barbara might make the trip. Aaron recognized an opportunity to make some extra money in the off-season while working on his hitting and establishing a position to play in the field. Their teammate Horace Garner stayed in Jacksonville to tend bar at Manuel's Tavern.

Playing ball in Puerto Rico during the winter of 1953 also kept Aaron from being drafted into military service. The war in Korea was over but the draft board in Mobile had already inducted the baseball-playing Bolling brothers and Aaron thought he could be next. When Caguas formally offered Aaron a roster spot for the winter, the Braves spoke on Aaron's behalf to the draft board. The possibility existed that Aaron might be involved in the integration of the Southern League, where they assumed he would be playing for the Atlanta Crackers during the upcoming season. The historical significance of this scenario was not lost on the draft board and Aaron did not hear from them again.

In Puerto Rico, Aaron continued to struggle at the second base position while hitting far below his standards after the first few weeks of the season. Caguas was managed by Hall-of-Fame catcher Mickey Owen, who came up with the idea of moving Aaron to the outfield.

I sent him out there and hit him some fly balls. He just turned and ran and caught them. I thought, well, he can catch the ball, but can he throw it? I'd never seen him throw anyway but underhanded. So I hit him some ground balls and told him to charge and throw them to second base. He threw the ball overhand, right to second base. Then I told him to cut loose and throw one to third. So he cut loose and that ball came across the infield as good as you ever saw. That was it. He was an outfielder.[1]

It all started to come together for Aaron that winter. Barbara gave birth to the couple's first child, Gaile, shortly after their arrival in Puerto Rico.

The Caguas team was loaded with black and Latino future major leaguers, including Charlie Neal, who replaced Aaron at second base and formed a more suitable double-play tandem with Mantilla. The two would later share infield responsibilities with the 1962 "Original Mets." Center field was occupied by "Jungle Jim" Rivera, and at first base was Vic Power, whom Aaron thought should have been the first black player for the New York Yankees. There were also some white Braves prospects wintering in Puerto Rico on their way to the big leagues; outfielder Dale Long and pitcher Bob Buhl both already had big league experience. Buhl was coming off a fantastic rookie season with the Braves, going 13–8 with a 2.97 ERA in 1953. Winter league play was more popular with players at all levels in the 1950s and 1960s than today, when they actually needed the extra money that could be earned in the off-season. Aaron began to feel comfortable in the outfield and his hitting returned to form against no less than major league caliber pitching. In the winter league, he was again named to the All-Star team, his fourth in four consecutive leagues, including the Negro League Indianapolis club. At the All Star Game, played in Caguas, Aaron hit two monstrous home runs over the center-field bleachers—400 feet from home plate. He finished the season with a .322 batting average, third best in the league, and tied Rivera for the home-run title with 9.

Once again Aaron captured not only the attention of coaches, teammates, and opponents but scouts for rival big league organizations as well. Tom Sheehan of the New York Giants gave his report on Aaron's winter-ball exploits to the Giants at their spring training facility in Phoenix at the beginning of the 1954 season: "Fellas, I've been feasting my eyes on a kid in the Caribbean who could just turn out to be a better player than Willie Mays. His name is Henry Aaron."[2]

At the conclusion of the winter league season, Aaron, Barbara, and the baby returned to Mobile for the few weeks that remained of the off-season. Following his own story through newspaper accounts, Aaron assumed he would be slated for the Braves Triple-A Toledo affiliate in Toledo, Ohio, or possibly teamed with Garner and Mantilla to integrate yet another league—the Southern—in Atlanta. But it was a different kind of "break" that gave Aaron his big chance that spring. On March 13, newly acquired outfielder Bobby Thomson—the same Bobby Thomson whose "shot heard 'round the world" for the New York Giants Aaron had listened to on the radio in that pool hall three years before— fractured his ankle during an exhibition game. The Braves had in February 1954 acquired Thomson, a three-time All-Star, in exchange for four players and $50,000 and he was a major part of their plans to compete for the National League pennant with the champion Brooklyn Dodgers. Despite winning ninety-two games in 1953, the Braves still finished a distant second behind a powerful Brooklyn club that had been the league's representative in the World Series for the last two seasons.

Aaron, who was still working on his conversion to an outfielder, felt every bit the 20-year-old minor leaguer that he was and had hardly considered that he would step in when Thomson went down. In fact, he was standing nearby, sipping Coca-Cola in a narrow breezeway beside the dugout on the third-base side when Thomson caught his leg in the dirt sliding into second following a hard line drive to left field. Thomson was carried off the field on a stretcher and right past Aaron through that same breezeway. Although Aaron was concerned and even distressed by the situation, he gave little consideration to its ramifications. Upon thinking it through, he figured the Braves would probably plug in Jim Pendleton, who hit .299 while playing more than one hundred games for the Braves in the outfield the previous season. Aaron wasn't even sure if the short time he had spent as outfielder had prepared him to handle the everyday duties of the position.

Just a few days earlier, Thomson had told Aaron he'd be better off not pursuing a spot in the outfield. "I told him to switch back to the infield; he would last longer there," Thomson was quoted in the newspaper.[3] Intimidated by the presence of so many big leaguers, Aaron had little idea how his recent winter league stint had made a lasting impression on all who witnessed it.

Aaron's winter league teammate Bob Buhl encouraged Hank to make his best effort at going after the position, and went as far as petitioning Braves manager Charlie Grimm to give Aaron a good look. The next day, Aaron was the starting left fielder against the Boston Red Sox in Sarasota. Aaron knocked a home run with such a crack that it drew none other than Ted Williams from the clubhouse to see who could hit a ball with such a thunderous clap. Williams, considered by many the greatest hitter of all time, never seemed to take a waking breath without thinking about hitting. He had no idea who the skinny kid was who had dared draw his attention with the sound of his bat.

I was playing in Sarasota, and because I was an older, more experienced player, I got to play the first three innings and then Boom! They take me out. I went in and showered and came on out because I wanted to watch the rest of the game. In Sarasota there was a nice little field and you had to go through a little dugout door and then sit on the bench. So I went out and just as I dove through the door, I hear WHACK!, and then the roar of the crowd—it was a small crowd but it was a helluva roar anyway—and one of my teammates said, "Did you see that guy hit that ball?"[4]

All eyes and ears were on Aaron that spring at the Braves camp in Bradenton; a tremendous amount of advance billing had preceded his arrival. Most news stories included a statistical recounting of his two minor league seasons and mentioned his Northern League Rookie of the Year and Sally League MVP awards. Although the stories are largely flattering in their praise for Aaron's talent and the high expectations for his future, many are peppered with offhanded racist epithets. References to negative racial stereotypes associated with Aaron's blackness are woven into the body of the stories, not only in the form of quotations from players and coaches, but by the writers of the stories who seem to have no consciousness or consideration of the slurs contained in their sentences. In "'Slow Motion' Aaron Becomes Colorful Figure in Braves Camp," a March 21, 1954, article in the *Milwaukee Journal*, teammate Joe Adcock and writer Sam Levy depict Aaron in what could easily be described as racist jargon: "The bewildered rookie of three weeks ago now acts like he is one of the gang. He smiles when Joe Adcock calls him 'Slow Motion Henry,' because of the way he shuffles on and off the field." Further down in the same story the mention of Aaron's race paints a picture analogous with the slave trading block: "Aaron's strongest critic is Dewey Griggs, a Braves scout on whose final recommendation the Negro was purchased."

While white players were certainly also "purchased," the use of racial modifiers such as Anglo or white did not precede references to their sales. Perhaps reporters may have thought the uniqueness or newness of the situation concerning African Americans called for such descriptive passages, but in retrospect the juxtaposition of the words "Negro was purchased" is striking in its imagery. In the paragraphs immediately following the stereotypical theme of the story is reinforced:

Likes Hot Weather
"The last day I watched Henry, he played in a double header and made seven hits," said Griggs. "He was an infielder then, and a good one. After the games, I called Aaron aside and told him that he

should show more pep on the field. Even when he threw a runner out, he did it in a slow motion manner."

Aaron looked at me for a few seconds. Then he said: "Mr. Griggs, my daddy told me long ago never hurry, son, unless you have to. Well, I've followed daddy's advice and here I am in the majors. Just give me a little more time to get acquainted. Then I'll show you lots of life. And that Adcock fellow won't call me Slow Motion. Besides, who can be peppy in 40 and 45 degree weather like this? I love to play when it's 100 in the shade."[5]

While this may have been a typical use of language at the time and the writers and speakers may have been oblivious to its offensive nature, it was not lost on Aaron who in retrospect described the feeling of being stigmatized.

I was in Bradenton, Florida, trying to make the club and convince everybody that I wasn't a lazy kid just off the cotton field, which is what they all seemed to think.

In those days, there was no problem with saying it either. . . . It wasn't regarded as bigotry for a white person to make lighthearted reference to a black person's laziness or ignorance. . . . I remember Charlie Grimm, calling me "Stepanfetchit" in the newspaper. It was in the headline of the *Milwaukee Journal*: "Aaron Has Nickname of Stepanfetchit, Because He Just Keeps Shuffling Along."[6]

Against this backdrop, a sequel to the Jacksonville experience, with all the same trappings of segregation, Aaron did keep "shuffling along." In an exhibition game against the New York Yankees, he blasted a ball over center fielder Irv Noren's head that went for a triple. The next time Aaron came to bat, Noren backed up some 415 feet from home plate, beyond what would normally be the extremity of the outfield fence in most big league ballparks.

Aaron hit two more home runs that spring, and finished the exhibition season batting over .300. In two weeks time, Aaron had proved himself and on the day before the Braves broke from camp in Bradenton, as Aaron was packing his duffel bag, manager Charlie Grimm tossed Hank his glove and said, "Kid you're my left fielder. It's yours until somebody takes it away from you."[7] At age 20, the minor leagues were behind him forever.

On April 1, 1954, in Mobile, Alabama, the Milwaukee Braves and Brooklyn Dodgers faced each other in the fourth game of an eight-game barnstorming tour of the south that the two teams played as they made their way north for Opening Day. Just as he had told his father six years before, Aaron had made it to the big leagues in time to play against Jackie Robinson. The series had begun in Florida and continued with stops in Mobile and Birmingham, Alabama, and Nashville and Chattanooga, Tennessee. In Mobile, Aaron banged a single and double in front of his family against his hero's team.

For the duration of the barnstorming tour, the black players on the Braves and Dodgers teams stayed at the same hotels separate from the white players. In the evenings, Aaron found his way to Jackie Robinson's room where a historic group of the first black major leaguers, including Don Newcombe, Roy Campanella, Joe Black, and Jim Gilliam, would also gather to play cards and discuss life on the big league road. Like a fly on the wall Aaron sat quietly and absorbed every bit of information he could about where to go, what to do and how to get along in the cites of the National League. The life lessons that Aaron learned in his initial barnstorming tour with the Dodgers became part of his makeup as a ballplayer and would help define the way he approached the game for the duration of his career as a player. "Those rooms were my college," he would later mention in his autobiography.[8]

During that fateful week, Aaron would receive a crash course on how to cope with the hostile situations he was sure to encounter. Every one of the black Dodgers players had already been in the eye of the storm; each had been spit at, spiked, teased, and tested. Each had been pushed to the limits of intestinal fortitude and restraint. In those rooms, Aaron and the players who were his opponents on the baseball field became teammates in a common struggle. They were lessons Aaron never forgot.

Dodgers pitcher Don Newcombe, who broke in with Brooklyn in 1949, was among the first dozen African Americans in the big leagues, and the first to pitch for the National League in the World Series. Many years later, Newcombe recalled the impact black players in the major leagues were having on American society at large: "We talked about what our state was, from 1947–1954. What we were going to do about things that were important to us. What we could do as a team or a group. We made significant strides in getting other civil rights people involved and interested in what we were doing."[9]

The great magnitude of what they were accomplishing individually and collectively regarding integration of the entire country was not lost on Aaron and the other black players of the late 1940s and early 1950s. Thrust into the center of the race relations arena, these young ballplayers, some of them still teenagers, acquired a social consciousness that viewed succeeding on the ballfield as part of a larger responsibility and as a contribution to a greater cause.

Just six weeks after Robinson's arrival in the major leagues in April of 1947, 23-year-old Larry Doby made his big league debut with the Cleveland Indians, a team owned by another baseball maverick named Bill Veeck. Doby was an All-Star second baseman for the Negro National League's Newark Eagles from

1942–1943 and 1946–1947, before and after serving in the military. Although Doby was four years younger than Robinson, he was a seasoned veteran who hit .341 in 1946 while leading his Newark team to the Negro World Series championship. He was the first player to go directly from the Negro Leagues to the major leagues, appearing in twenty-nine games in 1947. Upon Doby's arrival, owner Veeck gave the player some brief advice: "Just remember, they play with a little white ball and a stick of wood up here just like they did in your league."[10]

Amidst far less fanfare, Doby mirrored all the things Robinson symbolized, suffering the same indignities that Robinson faced but toiling in relative obscurity. Doby's experience is probably a more accurate representation of the early African American ballplayer's experience than the dramatic situation of Robinson, who was cast in the spotlight.

Doby played thirteen seasons in the major leagues, leading the American League in home runs twice and RBIs once, and was named to seven All-Star teams. In 1978, when Bill Veeck hired him to pilot the Chicago White Sox, Doby followed yet another Robinson—Frank—becoming only the second black manager in the majors. In 1998, the Veteran's Committee voted Doby into the National Baseball Hall of Fame.

On Opening Day 1954, Aaron was one of 13 new black players to arrive in the major leagues. Of the 16 major league teams, 12 were already integrated by a total of 38 black players, including Doby, Satchel Paige, Roy Campanella, and other future Hall-of-Famers like Monte Irvin (arriving in 1949), Willie Mays (1951), and Ernie Banks (1953).

Not coincidentally, the best teams in the major leagues, especially the National League, were the ones with more black players on their rosters, such as the Brooklyn Dodgers, the New York Giants, and Aaron's Braves. In 1954, the Braves, with Aaron, Bill Bruton, and Wes Covington, would field the first all-black outfield in the major leagues.

And black players in the early years of integration won many of baseball's major awards. Willie Mays became the fourth African American to win the Rookie of the Year Award since it was created in Robinson's honor in 1947. In fact, six of the first seven recipients of the award had previously played in the Negro Leagues. While it was certainly considered prestigious to be recognized as the best first-year player, it was almost ludicrous to consider experienced Negro League players to be rookies. The dominance with which African Americans with Negro League experience won the award during the breakthrough years could also be attributed to major league baseball casting itself in a light of superiority, creating the award in an almost condescending manner: players with Negro League experience, having played at similar if not equal levels of competition, were considered rookies as much as white players who had never stepped on a big league diamond.

In the second half of the 1950s, black players would win the National League MVP award with the same dominance. Aaron would be one of six black players to capture the NL MVP award in a seven-year stretch from 1956 to 1962. The barnstorming tour Aaron and the Braves made with the Dodgers during the days leading up to his first major league Opening Day served as his initiation into two fraternities, major league baseball and the brotherhood of its black players.

NOTES

1. Aaron, with Wheeler, *I Had a Hammer*, 77.
2. Musick, *Hank Aaron*, 54.
3. Red Thisted, "Rookie Aaron, 20, Makes Trial Run in Bobby's Shoes," *Milwaukee Journal*, March 24, 1954.
4. Aaron, with Dick Schaap, *Home Run*, ix.
5. Sam Levy, "'Slow Motion' Aaron Becomes Colorful Figure in Braves Camps," *Milwaukee Journal*, March 21, 1954.
6. Aaron, with Wheeler, *I Had a Hammer*, 85.
7. Aaron, with Bisher, *Aaron*, 49.
8. Aaron, with Wheeler, *I Had a Hammer*, 87.
9. Tollin, *Hank Aaron, Chasing the Dream*.
10. Larry Moffi and Jonathan Kronstadt, *Crossing the Line, Black Major Leaguers, 1947–1959* (Iowa City: University of Iowa Press, 1994), 16.

Aaron, Eddie Mathews, and Joe Adcock combined to hit more than 1,000 home runs together as teammates with the Milwaukee Braves from 1954–1962, the most by any group of three. Aaron and Mathews share the record for home runs by teammates, with a collective 863. *National Baseball Hall of Fame Library, Cooperstown, N.Y.*

"HAPPY DAYS" IN MILWAUKEE, 1954–1956

Aaron finished the spring exhibition season of 1954 in impressive fashion, knocking 4 hits in his last 8 at-bats in Nashville and Chattanooga, including 2 doubles and a triple with a pair of RBIs. Even though everyone else, including manager Charlie Grimm, had told him he was ticketed for the big leagues, Aaron was still not convinced: "I'd read stories about players being told that and then winding up playing left bar stool in Saginaw, Michigan."[1]

Aaron had been playing in exhibition games with the Braves big league club through the spring training season every day since Bobby Thomson broke his ankle, but General Manager John Quinn did not actually put a contract in front of him until the day before Opening Day. Six years after he told his father he would play in the majors against Jackie Robinson and twelve days after Herbert Aaron saw it for himself, Aaron signed on the line for $5,000 for one year.

One month to the day after Thomson broke his ankle, Aaron made his big league debut on Opening Day in Cincinnati. At the time and for many years to come, Cincinnati, home of the first professional baseball club, was the traditional locale for major league baseball's season opener. On such a day twenty years later, Aaron would again step into the batter's box wearing a visiting Braves uniform in Cincinnati, standing on the brink of breaking the most celebrated record in baseball history.

But on Opening Day 1954, Aaron was a 20-year-old rookie with no ideas about hitting more than 700 home runs over the next 20 years. Bud Podbielan, a journeyman pitcher who would go on to post a 25–42 record in nine big league seasons, was on the mound for the Reds. Although Aaron did not get a hit off him in his first big league at-bat, the rest of the Braves didn't seem to have any trouble. Podbielan was knocked out of the box by the second inning. It was a hitter's day for both teams. Aaron recalled chasing four balls hit by Cincinnati's Jim Greengrass that all bounced into the crowd for ground-rule doubles.

Joe Nuxhall came on in relief for the Reds in the second. Ten years earlier, Nuxhall had earned the distinction of being the youngest player in big league history when at age 15 he took the hill for the Reds against the National League champion St. Louis Cardinals. In his infamous first outing, Nuxhall looked good, retiring the first two batters he faced but couldn't shake the butterflies when Stan Musial stepped to the plate. A complete implosion ensued as Nuxhall couldn't get another out, surrendering five runs on two hits and five walks. He was socked out of the game and all the way back to the minor leagues. It took seven years for Nuxhall to finally get that next big league out, returning to the Reds in 1952. The Nuxhall that Aaron faced on Opening Day 1954 was a grizzled veteran not above playing hardball when he had to, and Aaron got an eyewitness lesson in what to look out for when a batter hits behind the team's best slugger in the line-up. Braves third baseman Eddie Mathews was beginning his third year with the team and had led the National League with 47 home runs in the previous season. Aaron remembered the game as follows:

> The first thing I learned was that Eddie Mathews was our money guy. He hit two home runs. The second thing I learned was what happens after a guy hits two home runs. I was on deck in the eighth inning when Andy Pafko, our cleanup hitter, came up against Nuxhall after Mathews's second homer, and I had a good view of Nuxhall's fastball crashing against Pafko's helmet. They took Pafko to the hospital, and the Reds won the game 9–8.[2]

Perhaps a little intimidated by watching Pafko get drilled and have his crumpled remains carried from the field, Aaron failed to get a hit in his final at-bat and finished his inauspicious debut going 0 for 5. However, he did manage to make history that day as reported in the *Sporting News* under the headline, "Rookie Aaron Sets All-Time Major First Alphabetically." The article explained that of the thousands of players who ever participated in a major league game, Henry Aaron's name would come first alphabetically. Previously the honor went to John Abadie, who according to the all-time register of players and managers in the *Baseball Encyclopedia*, played with the Philadelphia Centennials and the Brooklyn Athletics back in 1875 in the old National Association. (Fifty years later, Aaron would still be the first hitter listed in the register, although a pitcher named David Aardsma would join the ranks of major leaguers in 2004.)

After an off-day, the Braves resumed play with their home opener against the St. Louis Cardinals on April 15 in front of 39,963 anxious fans—reported by the *Sporting News* as "the largest crowd in Milwaukee history."[3] The game was one of the most highly anticipated in baseball history. Upon the announcement of the Braves impending move to Milwaukee, the baseball starved fans of Wisconsin had begun counting the minutes until this day.

In the game, Aaron collected his first major league hit, a double off former New York Yankees hurler Vic Raschi, a veteran of six World Series who was making his NL debut with the Cardinals. The Braves ran Raschi in the second inning en route to a 7–6 win behind Warren Spahn, who worked the 11-inning distance. Aaron was 2 for 5 and found a favorite target in Raschi, whom he would connect against one week later in St. Louis for his first big league home run.

In his memoir/homage, *Me and Hank*, author Sandy Tolan cited the work of local historian John Gurda to describe the mood of Milwaukee prior to its inaugural big league season. According to Gurda, "The reaction of Wisconsin residents bordered on hysteria." On a Sunday in March 1953, after learning that the Braves would be moving from Boston, "nearly 60,000 people drove out to County Stadium just to watch the grass grow . . . as many as 15,000 fans showed up before every game to cheer infield practice. Comparable crowds formed at Union Station or Mitchell Field to welcome the team home from routine road trips. The players were showered with beer, cheese, sausage, clothing, pens, and jewelry." The black Braves were no exception.[4]

The exuberance and absolute euphoria the fans in Milwaukee felt for their baseball team was an ideal example of American life in the 1950s and was employed twenty years later as the prototype for the nostalgic television series *Happy Days*. To a man, Aaron and his Braves teammates of the 1950s recall Milwaukee with the fondness of a first love. "Baseball has never seen fans like Milwaukee's in the 1950's and never will again," said Aaron.[5]

Pitcher Lew Burdette joined the Braves one year before Aaron in 1953, the team's first in Milwaukee. During his eleven seasons with the club, Burdette won 188 games, became a World Series hero by beating the New York Yankees three times in 1957, and was a perennial fan favorite. "I don't think we had to pay for anything in Milwaukee except for produce and soap products. We had a new car to drive, gasoline, laundry dry cleaning," recalled Burdette.[6]

Warren Spahn had been with the Braves in Boston for eight years before the team moved. He won 234 of his 363 career victories in Milwaukee, leading the

National League in wins six out of nine years from 1953 to 1962, including five in a row from 1957 to 1961. "I don't think we would have gotten arrested if we ever did anything bad in Milwaukee," said Spahn.[7]

Future commissioner of major league baseball Bud Selig was a prominent member of the Milwaukee business community at the time; his family owned an auto dealership that would lend cars to Braves players. Years later, after the Braves left for Atlanta following the 1965 season, Selig would be behind the push to bring baseball back to Milwaukee in the form of the Milwaukee Brewers. But in the 1950s, he was a fan above everything else, one of the more than 2.1 million—a National League attendance record—who came to Braves games in 1954. As Selig remembered, "There was a freshness, there was a sincerity, there was a love affair. It didn't matter if you were black or white. You were a Milwaukee Brave and you were young and you were good and the community loved you and it was what it was supposed to be."[8]

The warm welcome and enthusiastic response received by Aaron and his teammates, black and white, made Aaron feel that "Milwaukee was a million miles away from the Jim Crow south." And forty years later, Aaron's first wife, Barbara Lucas, recalled the city fondly. "Milwaukee is a baseball town, you have to understand. They don't care if you were black, white, yellow, green or purple as long as you were winning," said Lucas. Life itself was easier in the big leagues as well. Gone were the days of sleeping in a sitting up position on overnight bus rides and stretching two-dollars-a-day meal money into a week's worth of bologna sandwiches. "Happy days," recalled Lucas, "Milwaukee days were happy days."[9]

In the third game of the 1954 season, Aaron doubled to go 1 for 2 in a 5–1 Braves win at home against Cincinnati. He went 0 for 3 and 1 for 4 in a doubleheader the next day giving him a 4 for 19 (.210) start in the first four games.

For perhaps the first time in his professional career, Aaron was not the best player in his league or even on his team. From an offensive standpoint, that honor belonged to Eddie Mathews, who was emerging as one of the league's premier sluggers. In the 1940s in Boston, the popular catchphrase about the Braves was "Spahn and Sain and pray for rain," as the Dynamic Duo of Warren Spahn and Johnny Sain combined to compile most of the Braves victories. For the new Braves, Spahn and Burdette was as formidable a pair to be found on any National League roster. One year ahead of Aaron, Bill Bruton was the Braves first African American player and immediately endeared himself to the Milwaukee faithful, capturing an eternal place in their hearts with a game-winning eleventh inning home run in the Braves inaugural opener.

Aaron roomed with Jim Pendleton, whom he beat out for a starting spot in the outfield during spring training, and was taken under the wing of Bruton.

Pendleton was a free wheeling, free spending ladies man, who Aaron remembers as cashing his checks at bars on the road and leaving the money as a line of credit; he was a guy who may or may not have returned to the room on any given night. Conversely, Bruton was a model citizen and family man. All the black players on the Braves referred to Aaron as their little brother but Bruton actually watched over Henry and navigated the way for the others as well, making transportation arrangements and securing restaurant reservations for black players who still could not eat with their white teammates.

Milwaukee may have been "Baseball Heaven" for all the Braves, but the rest of the National League cities were mostly uncharted, segregated territories and quite possibly hostile environments for unfamiliar black faces. Cincinnati, the birthplace of professional baseball, was particularly notorious in its treatment of Aaron, Bruton, Pendleton, any other black players in the National League and African Americans in general. Restaurants in the hotels where the team stayed were unavailable to blacks, and other places that may not have posted signs stating their policies of not serving blacks would simply ignore would-be black patrons until they left.

Seven years after Jackie Robinson and Larry Doby began making regular appearances in National and American League cities, black players who could be plainly seen on the field often went unrecognized elsewhere. Author Ralph Ellison described this experience in the prologue to his literary classic *Invisible Man*, which was first published in 1952: "Like the bodiless heads you see sometimes in circus sideshows, it is as though I have been surrounded by mirrors of hard, distorting glass. When they approach me they see only my surroundings, themselves, or figments of their imagination—indeed, everything and anything except me."[10]

One surefire way for Aaron to be noticed away from the baseball diamond was to travel in the company of a white woman. In Cincinnati, Aaron, on an off-day, visited with a friend who had married an Italian woman. She had brought her sister along and the four were driving in a car in the neighboring town of Covington, Kentucky, when they were pulled over by a policeman who asked if Aaron was married to the woman he was sitting next to in the car. When Aaron explained that he was just traveling with friends, he was told by the police officer to get out of the car and out of town as well; in Covington, the officer declared, black men didn't travel with white women.

St. Louis was just as bad. Dodgers pitcher Don Newcombe, who had spent 1952–1953 with the U.S. military during the Korean War, was angered upon returning to find that even after serving his country in the army he was still not allowed to stay in the Adams Hotel in St. Louis with his Dodgers teammates. He and Robinson took their grievance to the hotel's manager and eventually gained admittance for all the National League's black players, though the restaurant remained off-limits.

While Aaron continued to learn about the relative civility with which he and others were treated throughout the National League's cities, the rest of the nation was about to get its first lesson in civil rights. Almost two years after first hearing the argument of a Topeka, Kansas, man whose eight-year old daughter walked twenty-one blocks to school every morning when there was another school much closer to home, the Supreme Court pronounced its ruling in the landmark *Brown v. Board of Education* case on May 17, 1954.

Seven years after baseball initiated its integration, the *Brown* decision legally compelled the United States to tear away the "separate but equal" façade behind which institutionalized racism had been hiding. The painful process of desegregating the nation's schools had begun and the Civil Rights movement was up and running. Back in Aaron's home state of Alabama, a 10-year-old future leader of the Civil Rights movement named John Lewis was attending a segregated public school in Pike County. Aaron and Lewis would cross paths many years later in Atlanta where Aaron's Braves would move and Lewis would become a congressman for the state of Georgia. Although the *Brown* decision represents the birth of the Civil Rights movement, progress, in society as in professional baseball, was slow.

"The decision created a great deal of excitement, a great deal of hope, a great deal of optimism. It created a climate that said, 'we can fight, there is a better way to bring about a better society.' But it didn't happen," said Lewis.[11]

Despite the hospitality Milwaukee bestowed on the Braves, Aaron was still subject to subtle racial discrimination. Eleven years after his rookie season, on the eve of the Braves impending move South, Aaron visited Atlanta for a precursory examination of the city's living conditions and compared them to Milwaukee.

"Actually, Atlanta is not south," he told a *Milwaukee Journal* sportswriter. "What I mean is, it isn't like the rest of the south. The only thing bad about it is it happens to be in Georgia. They have made tremendous progress in all phases. The Negroes there are way ahead of the Negroes here. It's no contest. Sure they've got segregation problems there but they've got them in Milwaukee, too. Up here they call it 'de facto segregation.' Down there they just call it segregation."[12]

Aaron received his first lesson in de facto segregation when he tried to buy his first house in Milwaukee. He made a handful of attempts at moving into different suburbs of the city only to be passed around by white realtors like a hot potato. After visiting the northwestern Milwaukee suburb of Mequon to speak to a Boy Scout group at the request of a local black realtor and friend named Tom Cheeks, Aaron became attracted to the neighborhood. He asked Cheeks to help him find a place to live in the area. When a white builder realized he would be selling to a black man, he requested that the sale be made first to the real estate office and then to Aaron so that the builder could avoid being directly responsible for the sale. "The builder was afraid of criticism for selling to minorities," Cheeks later told *Me and Hank* author Sandy Tolan, adding that Aaron's new neighbors had called Cheeks at home to lodge complaints as soon as they found out Aaron was moving in.[13]

Aaron's daughter, Gaile, was the only black child at her Mequon grade school. Although she was quick to make new friends of many of her white classmates, she was also subject to racially inspired abuse, such as having her boots slit with a razor while riding on the school bus. The story of Aaron's younger sister, Alfredia, is more matter of fact than de facto. Alfredia was so excited about her brother being in the big leagues, she convinced her mother Estella to let her move to Milwaukee and live with Hank and Barbara. She also attended grade school in Mequon but moved back to Alabama when the rough treatment she received not only from students but also from teachers and administrators became too much. After breaking down one day at the breakfast table and telling her older brother about the situations she had been enduring, Aaron and his wife Barbara decided to pay a visit to the school's principal. Alfredia recalled the principal saying, "There wouldn't be a problem if you hadn't brought her to this school."[14]

Aaron and the Braves arrived in Milwaukee as the city was in transition. Traditionally inhabited by Polish and German immigrants, Milwaukee had recently experienced a large migration of blacks from the south seeking work in the growing industries of foundries and tanneries. Former Mayor Frank Zeidler told author Sandy Tolan that "it was like two galaxies coming together."[15]

Despite progress, pockets of resistance to change held fast and surfaced in the more blatant forms of racism Aaron encountered. However, according to Zeidler, Aaron's arrival at this crucial juncture in Milwaukee's history also encouraged progress in race relations by forcing whites to recognize the abilities and accomplishments of blacks, with African American accomplishment on the baseball diamond as a primary example.

While Milwaukee continued to come to terms with its developing identity, and Aaron for the most part seemed to be welcomed by the city, he was occasionally subject to overt racist treatment from his own Braves teammates. Sometimes consciously, sometimes unconsciously, sometimes with deliberate intent and sometimes inadvertently, some of the Braves biggest stars were also its biggest bigots. In his *I Had a Hammer* autobiography, Aaron spoke of pitcher Lew Burdette's reputation for directing derogatory remarks and pitches at black players. In fact, before Jim Pendleton became a teammate of his, Burdette had beaned him when they played against each other in the minor leagues. Whatever the motivation for Burdette's behavior, Aaron at least was aware of it. If an opposing pitcher threw at any of the Braves black players, Burdette, keeping with protocol, would retaliate; Aaron said he could not assume the other Braves pitchers would do the same. At least Aaron knew where Burdette stood. Likewise with outfielder Joe Adcock, who, during an accidental encounter while the two occupied bathroom stalls next to each other in the clubhouse, Aaron overheard using racial epithets in reference to scouting a black ballplayer. When the pair emerged from their stalls at the same time, Adcock realized what he had said and offered an apology. Whether this behavior was ingrained in their personalities or something major league baseball had instilled in white players like Burdette and Adcock, at least it was recognizable. What was more offensive to Aaron were the subtler types of remarks masked in the form of jokes by the Braves team leader and most boisterous locker room prankster Warren Spahn. A veteran with the Braves for a decade in Boston before the move to Milwaukee, Spahn used his status as the team's elder statesman to speak his mind freely. Aaron remembered a pair of particularly insensitive quips, one an oft-repeated line attributed to Spahn that went: "What's black, has six legs and catches flies? The Braves outfield." The other concerned a time Spahn pointed to a cockroach lying on its back on the floor and said, "Hey Doc, come over here and turn Hank over."

Many years later Spahn offered an explanation but still seemed unable to understand the offensive nature of his dialogue.

> I was referring to the fact that it was just laying there motionless more than I was to the color, because we used to tease Hank about how slowly he moved. . . . You know when I came into baseball in the forties, we'd call an Italian a Dago, and a German like me was a Flathead or a Hardhead. But when Jackie Robinson came into the league, he had immunity. You couldn't say anything toward the color of a man's skin. I think Jackie took advantage of that. Jackie got arrogant after a while. Then Campanella came along, and some of the others and by the time Hank got there, the groundwork was broken.[16]

Attitudes towards race like Spahn's were not just prevalent but inherent in professional baseball and American society through to the 1950s. To its credit, baseball did give the Civil Rights movement a push, but many of the crossover players whose careers began before the time of integration lacked an understanding in areas of civility. The "groundwork" had indeed been "broken by the time Hank got there." Spahn and the others would have to get used to black players and refrain from directing derogatory language at them based on their ethnicity or skin color. It's possible that the status quo was threatened by the arrival of black players simply because of their abilities. Robinson won the first Rookie of the Year award, named in his honor in 1947, and the NL MVP award in 1949. Campanella won the MVP award in 1951 and 1953 and would again in 1955. The best player in the National League in 1954 was Willie Mays, whose Giants emerged on top after a season-long pennant chase with the Dodgers and Braves.

In the four years since Mays broke in, he had become baseball's biggest star and, even though Aaron was still green and wet-behind-the-ears, the comparisons that would be drawn between he and Mays for the duration of their careers had already begun. Mays topped the league in 1954 with a .345 batting average and 41 home runs and made his legendary catch in the Giants World Series victory over Cleveland. It would take a few years for Aaron to begin closing the gap between the two of them.

Aaron's 1954 season came to an abrupt halt in ironic fashion when he broke his ankle sliding into third base the same way Bobby Thomson's spring injury presented Aaron with the opportunity to crack the Braves Opening Day roster. It was Bobby Thomson who came in to pinch run for Aaron on September 5; the hit was Aaron's fifth of the day and his last of the season.

Overall, 1954 was a solid rookie campaign for Aaron who hit .280, higher than all but 27 of the National League's regular players, with 13 home runs, 69 RBIs, and 131 hits in 122 games. Aaron finished second in Rookie of the Year balloting behind outfielder Wally Moon of St. Louis, who hit .304 in 148 games.

Aaron earned the confidence of manager Charlie Grimm, whom he credited with having the courtesy to deliver his criticisms of Aaron's play in private. "If he had bawled me out in front of all those veterans we had at the time, there's no telling what would have happened to me, because in your first year you're scared all the time anyway."[17]

Aaron also received accolades from his peers. "We were skeptical at first when we heard that the kid would be in spring training with us," said Bobby Thomson. "But it was obvious right away that he was in a class by himself. He whipped that bat like a demon. He always hit line drives, even on home runs. Those drives shot off his bat as if they were from a cannon. We knew we were seeing one of the next greats in baseball."[18]

The broken ankle turned into a good break one a year later when the steel pin inserted in his leg made him ineligible for the draft. It also meant he couldn't go barnstorming with a team of Negro League veterans that included Jackie

Robinson, Don Newcombe, Monte Irvin, Larry Doby, Minnie Minoso, and Willie Mays.

Aaron spent the off-season playing with his baby daughter Gaile and driving around in his new Pontiac convertible. He reported early for spring training in 1955—too early; he and several other Braves were fined by the office of baseball commissioner Ford Frick. When the issue arose later and manager Charlie Grimm asked Aaron about the notification letter he had received regarding his fine, the story goes that Aaron's response to Grimm was to ask, "Who's Ford Frick?" The incident is at the center of the early development of Aaron's image as a slow-moving, slow-talking, unworldly country bumpkin, an image propagated by Grimm, who enjoyed spinning yarns for entertainment's sake, and perpetuated by others. "His stories about me contributed to an image that I'm still trying to shake," said Aaron. Another story out of spring training in 1955 had Aaron not knowing the identity of pitchers he had faced during exhibition games. "What they didn't say in the paper was that I knew what they all threw, and how hard, and where their release points were. I might not have had the names and words the way the sportswriters did, but I had a mental capacity at home plate that nobody seemed to appreciate."[19]

Before Opening Day 1955, the Braves publicity director and traveling secretary Donald Davidson acceded to Aaron's earlier request for a double-digit uniform number and assigned him 44. Davidson stood less than four feet tall and was himself subject to a lot of teasing, taunting, and outright discrimination, to which he responded with his own rants and tirades. Over the years, Aaron and Davidson developed a close personal relationship, which Aaron attributed to the fact that both had endured similar forms of prejudice. Aaron recalled a time when the pair was seated together at a restaurant where the waitress refused to serve Aaron. Davidson saw to it that the team never ate there again. Receiving the new number gave Aaron a stronger feeling of belonging and renewed confidence. In retrospect it almost seems prophetic that he would hit 44 home runs in four different seasons, leading the league three times with that total.

Aaron improved on every aspect of his game and all statistical categories in 1955, raising his batting average 34 points from the previous season to a fifth best in the league .314. He also began a record streak of 20 consecutive seasons of 20 or more home runs with 27. His 106 RBIs was the first of 11 seasons in which he eclipsed the century mark and his 105 runs scored was the first of 13 straight seasons over 100. He was also named to his first of 22 consecutive All Star Games, a streak spanning the duration of his career.

The Braves finished a distant second, thirteen-and-one-half games behind the Brooklyn Dodgers, who finally beat their cross-town rivals, the Yankees, in the World Series that year. An aging Jackie Robinson stole home in the first game, setting the pace for the Dodgers first World Series victory over the Yankees in six tries since 1941. If not quite in awe, Aaron still admired his boyhood heroes, the Dodgers, and admitted to taking a fan's interest in the team of 1955.

After the season, Aaron was back on the barnstorming circuit with the Negro League alumni team originally formed by Robinson, taken over by Campanella, and then by Mays, with whom Aaron, Monte Irvin, and Larry Doby formed the team's outfield. Ernie Banks played shortstop and Campanella was the catcher, with George Crowe, Hank Thompson, and Junior Gilliam rounding out the infield. Don Newcombe, Joe Black, Sam Jones, and Brooks Lawrence formed the pitching staff of a team that Aaron can't remember ever losing to the team of current Negro League stars that toured with them. "I don't think it would have mattered who we played. That might have been the best team ever assembled. I know I never saw a better one," said Aaron.[20]

At the end of the 1955 season, Aaron was named the Braves Most Valuable Player and received a hike in pay to $17,000 for the 1956 season. This was more money than Aaron thought he would ever make. Still, in the off-season, he took a job with the recreation department back in Mobile as a youth athletic instructor at Carver Park. He arrived for spring training in excellent physical condition and predicted he would improve his batting average in 1956. "I should hit 15 points better next year because I know the pitchers better and have lots more confidence in myself," said Aaron.[21]

Aaron missed his mark by one point but still managed to lead the National League with a .328 average. The Braves and Aaron both got off to a slow start and on June 17, with the team's record at 24–22, manager Charlie Grimm was fired and replaced by Fred Haney, who was described by Aaron as a stern and sometimes cantankerous disciplinarian.

In one of the first games with Haney at the helm, Aaron was accused by his new manager of not hustling hard enough to first base after hitting a ground ball off New York Giants pitcher Ruben Gomez. Haney administered a verbal tongue-lashing immediately following the play—in full view of Aaron's teammates. This made a less than favorable first impression with Aaron, who confronted Haney, explaining to his new manager that he didn't think he was above being criticized or even being yelled at but thought having it happen in front of the rest of the club could be counterproductive and would most likely not produce the desired results. Aaron said the two never had any personal problems afterwards, and the Braves reeled off a string of eleven consecutive victories and fifteen wins in a stretch of seventeen games that catapulted the team from fifth to first place. The Braves remained at the top of the National League standings for most of the season, but sputtered down the stretch in September and clung to a mere one-game lead over the Dodgers, with the Cincinnati Reds lurking right behind. With three games left to play, the Braves traveled to St. Louis while the Dodgers hosted Pittsburgh. When Milwaukee dropped its first two to St. Louis and Brooklyn took the first pair from Pittsburgh, it was all over no matter what happened the next day. The Braves finished one game behind the Dodgers and received a final collective lambasting from Haney, who thereby served warning of the hell there would be to pay next spring.

As hard as he was on his players, Haney's record with the Braves was remarkable. He took over a floundering, underachieving club in fifth place two weeks before the season's midpoint and brought them to the brink of the World Series, posting a 68–40 mark since his takeover. In Haney's next three full seasons as manager, the Braves finished in first place twice and second once. Aaron and Haney developed a relationship over that time based on mutual admiration and respect.

While still basically a player who preferred to let his playing speak for itself, especially in the formative years of his professional playing days, Aaron also developed a reputation of quietly coexisting with his managers throughout his career.

> Of all the managers I've played for I've had no trouble with any of them. I think anytime you see friction between players and a manager, it's usually "fringe" ballplayers, players who are looking for an excuse and somebody to blame. They'll say things like, "The reason I didn't have a good season is he didn't pitch me every four days. Or he didn't let me play regularly."[22]

The only fringe Aaron was on in 1956 was the edge of baseball's elite class. He racked up league-leading totals with 200 hits, 34 doubles, and 340 total bases. His .558 slugging percentage (total bases divided by times at bat) tied him for third place with NL Rookie of the Year Frank Robinson (who burst on the scene in dramatic fashion knocking a rookie record 38 home runs). Aaron's 106 runs scored were also third best in the league and one up from the year before. His 26 home runs were one less than the previous year and his 92 RBIs were also down from 1955, a matter of no small concern to Aaron. "Those runs batted in . . . that's what I'm aiming for. They seem more important than your batting average. When you have a lot of RBIs, you know you're doing something for your team," said Aaron.[23]

At 22, Aaron was the second youngest player in the history of the National League to capture the batting title. Although Dodgers pitcher Don Newcombe won the league's MVP award and the first ever Cy Young Award, the *Sporting News* named Aaron its National League Player of the Year. The Dodgers lost the

1956 World Series in seven games to the Yankees in Jackie Robinson's final season in the majors.

On the baseball side, Jackie was still a consummate ballplayer and both a student and teacher of the game. Aaron recalled an occasion during the 1956 season in which Robinson was playing third base for the Dodgers at Ebbets Field and Aaron feigned a bunt which Robinson made no move to field. Afterwards, Aaron asked Jackie why he didn't come in to field the possible bunt. Robinson told Aaron a bunt was his last worry when a power hitter such as Aaron was at the plate. Robinson's words were a vote of confidence that Aaron carried with him to the batter's box thereafter.

NOTES

1. Musick, *Hank Aaron*, 62.
2. Aaron, with Wheeler, *I Had a Hammer*, 89.
3. R. L. Davids, "Rookie Aaron Sets All-Time Major First Alphabetically," *Sporting News*, April 28, 1954.
4. Sandy Tolan, *Me and Hank: A Boy and His Hero, Twenty-Five Years Later* (New York: Free Press, 2000), 85.
5. Tollin, *Hank Aaron, Chasing the Dream*.
6. Ibid.
7. Ibid.
8. Ibid.
9. Ibid.
10. Ralph Ellison, *Invisible Man* (New York: Random House, 1952; Quality Paperback Book Club edition, 1994), 3.
11. Tollin, *Hank Aaron, Chasing the Dream*.
12. Tolan, *Me and Hank*, 83.
13. Ibid., 84.
14. Aaron, with Wheeler, *I Had a Hammer*, 131.
15. Ibid., 94.
16. Ibid., 102.
17. Musick, *Hank Aaron*, 66.
18. Baldwin and Jenkins, *Bad Henry*, 61.
19. Aaron, with Wheeler, *I Had a Hammer*, 96.
20. Ibid., 106.
21. William Furlong, "The Panther at the Plate," *New York Times Magazine*, September 21, 1958, 48.
22. Cohen, *Hammerin' Hank of the Braves*, 49.
23. Musick, *Hank Aaron*, 72.

WHEN DREAMS COME TRUE, 1957

The military style boot camp manager Fred Haney had promised began on the first day of spring training in 1957. "'Gentlemen, the first thing I want you to realize is that we're here for one purpose—to get in shape,' he [Haney] said. By the time the season opens, you're going to be ready to play ball. Anybody got any questions?"[1] Nobody did.

In addition to the regular baseball practice drills, Haney ran his troops through a series of calisthenics that included push-ups, sit-ups, and a relentless amount of running. Intrasquad games were regularly interrupted if any kind of mistake was made. An error on a ground ball, a missed cutoff man, or even a pitcher giving up a home run was considered a mistake and the entire team would drop their gloves, bats or whatever else they were doing and run an entire lap around the ballpark.

"I won't say that spring training, 1957, was like running for the Boston Marathon. I never ran in the Boston Marathon. But I got a pretty good idea of how I'd train if I were planning to run in the Boston Marathon. I'd get Fred Haney to get me in shape like he got the Braves in shape in 1957," said Aaron.[2]

If Haney's methods were extreme, the Braves were up to the task. To a man, the disappointing conclusion of the 1956 season created a hunger in the bellies of the Braves who had collectively spent the longest winter of their careers pondering what might have been. "We were there to practice being perfect," Aaron said. "I don't think I ever saw a team open a season as determined to win the pennant."[3] Haney's military mentality caused his players to nickname him "Little Napoleon."

In Joel Cohen's 1973 book *Hammerin' Hank of the Braves*, a biography for young readers, the author quoted Aaron as saying he had never had any trouble with any of his managers. However, years later in his own autobiography, *I Had a Hammer*, Aaron mentioned having philosophical differences with Haney.

> I never quite figured Haney out. On one hand, he was a military man, very concerned with fitness and motivation. . . . On the other hand, I sometimes thought that after he got us in shape, Haney didn't do much managing at all—that he more or less let the team run itself. Maybe that was his philosophy. But I didn't go along with most of his methods and never really warmed up to him.[4]

Regardless of the relationship Aaron had with Haney, the time the two spent together in Milwaukee can best be described as the team's glory years and some of Aaron's most productive seasons, especially 1957, which unfolded like a dream come true.

Aaron relished his position as the National League's leading hitter from the previous season and he took great pride in overhearing Haney's description of him to newspaper reporters as potentially one of baseball's best right-handed batters. "Aaron is more like Hornsby than any hitter I ever saw," Haney said. "And Rogers Hornsby was the greatest right handed hitter I ever saw. It is incredible the way that kid can hit the ball to right with all that power. And he's more than just a natural hitter. He has the temperament and disposition to go with it."[5]

In the *Milwaukee Sentinel*, Red Thisted described the scoring in the Braves 4–1 victory over the Cubs in front of a sparse crowd of 23,674 at Wrigley Field in Chicago on Opening Day: "Henry Aaron, the 1956 batting champ, whistled a single to left. Mathews drilled a triple down the right field line for the tying tally and Adcock's hit registered Mathews with the tying marker. After Bobby Thomson fanned, Logan rammed a Rush pitch into the centerfield bleachers."[6]

In his first autobiography written with Furman Bisher, Aaron later recalled the feeling of accomplishment he had at the time and the eager anticipation with which the team approached each game of the 1957 season: "Ah, 'the 1956 batting champ' was a line I have to admit I sort of rolled around in my mind a little. I liked the sound of it. It represented one ambition achieved, but I had something more in my mind. At least we got a start like we didn't want to have to look back to see if anybody was gaining on us."[7]

Warren Spahn pitched a four-hit complete game in the opener and the Braves burst out of the gates winning nine of the team's first ten games. The Dodgers were just as hot and the Braves first loss of the season landed them in a tie for first place with Brooklyn. For his part, Aaron batted around .400 during the first few weeks. But by mid-May, both he and the Braves were slumping and Haney called the club to task, citing the team's September swoon of the previous season. *Milwaukee Sentinel* reporter Red Thisted singled out Aaron in one of his columns: "It is a little unfair to fault Henry Aaron individually for the recent string of defeats but it may as well be admitted now that when Henry isn't swishing that bat with authority, the Braves are in trouble. He has made two hits in the last 14 appearances and driven in one run in that time."[8]

Aaron accepted full responsibility for his contribution or lack thereof to the team's production. "If you're going to be the big man on your ball club, you've got be able to carry your load. This was one of the first times I can remember reading any story that said in effect, 'As Aaron goes, so go the Braves.' So I've got to say I liked it," said Aaron.[9]

Writers weren't the only ones aware of Aaron's status in the Braves line-up; opposing pitchers were paying recognition in their own particular way. While it may not have been Aaron's favorite form of flattery, the regularity with which pitchers were throwing at Henry was surely a sign that he had arrived. Because of resulting consequences, such as putting runners on base and possible ejection, pitchers are only allotted a certain amount of purpose pitches. Although such pitches were formerly reserved for sluggers Adcock and Mathews as well as for hitters who may have followed them in the order, Aaron, who had spent the first half of the season batting second in the line-up, was receiving more than his fair share of the bean ball distribution. Either Adcock or Mathews had been the Braves leading home run hitters for the previous five seasons; Mathews amassed a total of 190 over the period, drawing speculation that he might some day challenge the all-time record. But a changing of the guard was at hand and as Aaron moved into prominence as one of the National League's most prolific sluggers, hurlers adjusted their strategies on how to pitch to him. Twenty-year-old Don Drysdale of the Brooklyn Dodgers was a hard throwing up-and-comer one year removed from his rookie season; he would over the years earn a reputation for intimidation in the form of high, hard inside pitching. One night in Brooklyn, Drysdale threw two consecutive pitches up and in on Aaron that left no doubt as to their intent. After the game, Aaron was quoted as saying, "It didn't bother me. That punk doesn't throw hard enough to hurt me."[10] The comment touched off a rivalry between the two that would last for the duration of their careers. Adcock warned Aaron that talking to reporters about bean balls would only draw more fire.

For a while, it appeared that Drysdale's intimidation tactics were getting the best of Aaron who struggled in their early confrontations, so much so that Haney had considered benching him for one of Drysdale's scheduled starts. Aaron begged his way back into the line-up and after striking out in his first two at bats, eventually connected for a pair of base hits. After that, Aaron never had any trouble hitting Drysdale; in fact, he would go on to hit more home runs (17) off Drysdale than any other pitcher over the course of his entire big league career. Aaron had grown accustomed to being thrown at for reasons no simpler than the color of his skin before he had become a dominant slugger and never questioned whether Drysdale's inside pitching could have been racially motivated. The manner in which Drysdale threw at Braves batters, black and white, was indiscriminate. Drysdale's drilling of fiery Johnny Logan, who charged the mound after being knocked down by Drysdale, incited the biggest baseball brawl Aaron can recall.

As the 1957 season progressed, Aaron was among the league leaders in each of the Triple Crown categories, (home runs, RBIs, and batting average). Aaron's statistics prompted Milwaukee sportswriters to question manager Haney on why he was batting Aaron second in the order. Mathews was batting third, the spot generally reserved for a team's best hitter, with Adcock fourth and Bobby Thomson fifth. Mired in a season-long slump, Thomson was not producing the way a meat-of-the-order hitter should and was traded back to the New York Giants on June 15 for future Hall-of-Fame second sacker Red Schoendienst. The day before the trade, Haney had batted Aaron in the cleanup position and with no advance notice or any discussion Haney told Aaron that's where he'd stay. A short while after the trade, center fielder Bill Bruton and second baseman Felix Mantilla collided while running at full speed for a pop fly hit to short center field. The collision landed Mantilla on the bench for a month, put Bruton out for the season, and made Aaron his replacement in center field. Aaron did not exactly welcome the move; it was his third outfield spot in three seasons. Aaron started as a left fielder in 1954 when he filled in for Thomson. He moved to right the following year where he felt comfortable and remained except for a brief stint filling in for injured Danny O'Connell at second base in 1955. At the time of his move to center, Aaron was at or near the league lead in the three major hitting categories—batting near .340 with approximately 20 home runs and 55 RBIs.

On July 4, he knocked his 26th home run of the season prompting teammate Bruton to be the first to draw comparisons between Aaron and Babe Ruth. "Isn't it about time somebody started comparing Henry's home run record with Babe Ruth's the year he hit 60?"[11] The *Milwaukee Sentinel's* Lou Chapman did, discovering that Aaron was just two games behind Babe's pace.

Aaron felt uncomfortable in center field with Wes Covington in left field and newly acquired Bob "Hurricane" Hazle in right. Aaron had little confidence in the fielding ability of his outfield mates, and found the move to center field draining. Although he was still having the most prolific season of his career to date, his home run production and batting average dropped after his move to center field.

The Braves were in the thick of yet another tight pennant race, residing in first place for most of the season but closely pursued by Cincinnati and St. Louis. While Hazle may have been a defensive liability, he made up for it at the plate, hitting a whopping .403 with 7 home runs and 27 RBIs in 41 games down the stretch.

Aaron did not keep up the 60-homer pace, but he was still among the league leaders in the three major offensive categories and the big cog in the Braves machine. On August 15, he hit his 34th homer of the season off Don Gross in Cincinnati; the home run was also the 100th of his career—and he was still only 23 years old. The Braves rattled off a 10-game winning streak during August and pulled away from St. Louis and the rest of the pack to hold an 8½-game lead on September 3.

Meanwhile, as the sports pages chronicled the pennant race, race relations once again made front-page news. While Milwaukee fans continued to roll out in record numbers in support of a baseball team whose best player was black, 745 miles due south in Little Rock, Arkansas, the local government was not responding as favorably to the integration of its public institutions. The *New York Times* reported that Arkansas Governor Orval Faubus had deployed the state militia to keep black children from attending Little Rock Central High School's opening day, in defiance of an order from the federal district court. Fully armed, the troops kept the African American children from the school grounds while an angry crowd of 400 white men and women jeered, booed and shouted, "go home, niggers." Several hundred militiamen, with guns slung over their shoulders, carrying gas masks and billy clubs, surrounded the school.

Two years earlier, the Brooklyn Dodgers had considered having as many as eight black players on the team's roster, a prospect that prompted Dick Young of the *New York Daily News* to write, "I honestly don't believe baseball is ready for that step right now."[12]

The "Little Rock Nine" made it into Central High for half a day three weeks later, before a riot outside the school forced them to leave for their own safety. Two days later, they gained re-entry for the rest of the school year. It would be another 14 years before the Pittsburgh Pirates made history by becoming the first major league team to field a starting line-up of all black players on September 1, 1971.

As well as Aaron's first few seasons in the big leagues had gone, he couldn't understand the aversion of Young or anyone else to integrated baseball. "We never knew exactly what it was that white people were afraid of. The way we saw it, we were the ones who had reason to be afraid. We were the ones who could be arrested without a moment's notice. Or spiked, or beaned, or beaten, or shot or even hanged."[13]

By mid-September 1957, the Cardinals had at least one more comeback in them and, as the Braves lost eight of eleven games St. Louis, crept back into the race. By September 15, the Cardinals had whittled the Braves lead to two-and-one-half games.

The tension of the tight race cast a visible pall over moody manager Haney. Shortstop Johnny Logan asked Aaron if he noticed how pale Haney was getting. To which Aaron replied, "You think he's sick?" "I think we're all sick," Aaron recalled Logan saying. "How bad do you want to win this pennant?" "That's a crazy question," Aaron said. "All of us want to win it bad."[14]

Logan reminded Aaron of how the Braves fell just one game short the year before and speculated if they did not capture the NL flag this time Haney might not be back as manager next year. Although Aaron had never felt much sympathy for Haney, that night he began to see him in a different light.

"Don't get me wrong," Aaron later recalled. "I wasn't feeling any more for Haney than I was for myself, but suddenly I wanted to win the pennant worse than anything. I don't know how many others began to feel the same way, or if Logan even talked to any of the rest about it, but the next day we began to win again."[15]

Once again, the Braves caught fire, winning seven in a row as they approached the potential clincher. On September 22 against Chicago, Aaron tied Cubs shortstop Ernie Banks for the league lead in home runs with his 42nd. The next day, the Cardinals would come to Milwaukee for a three-game series with the Braves, who needed just one victory to clinch the pennant.

More than 40,000 people packed County Stadium in anticipation of the Braves clinching with a victory in the first game. Lew Burdette took the mound for the Braves opposed by Wilmer "Vinegar Bend" Mizell, who Aaron and Adcock reached for singles in the second inning. Andy Pafko beat out a bunt single to load the bases, and Aaron scored from third when Cardinals outfielder Wally Moon dropped a Wes Covington fly ball. Mizell was lifted for reliever Larry Jackson who succeeded in putting out the fire. The Cardinals took the lead scoring two runs off Burdette in the sixth. The Braves tied the score manufacturing a run in the seventh on a single by Schoendienst, a sacrifice bunt from Logan, and a double by Mathews. Reliever Billy Muffet replaced Jackson in the ninth and Gene Conley came on for the Braves in the top of the eleventh with the score still tied 2–2. Johnny Logan connected for a single off Muffet in the bottom of the eleventh and Eddie Mathews flied out bringing Aaron to the plate with one out and one aboard.

Looking for a curveball, Aaron got it on the first pitch. He laid the fat part of the bat into the ball for one of his patented tee-shots that everyone who saw and heard it knew was heading out of the park. With one swing, Aaron had clinched the pennant for the Braves. As he accelerated excitedly around the bases, visions of Bobby Thomson's blast to beat the Dodgers in 1951 danced in his head. In the back of his mind, he could hear the radio in the pool hall back in Mobile and seconds later his Braves teammates were carrying him off the field just like Thomson's teammates had six years before. Of the 755 regular season home runs Aaron would hit in his career none, not even 714 or 715 would mean as much to him as number 109 that clinched Milwaukee's first pennant. Aaron called the euphoric hours that followed a blur.

> I can remember all the players standing around a big table in the clubhouse after the game stuffing themselves with ribs and chicken and shrimp. I told the writers that for the first time in my life, I was excited. What I meant was that for the first time I felt like I could let down my guard and really act excited. I've never had another feeling like that. When I broke Babe Ruth's home run record, I was more relieved than excited. But this was as good as I knew how to feel.[16]

The excitement had barely subsided by the next day when a photograph of Aaron being carried off the field by his teammates shared space on the *Wisconsin CIO News* front page with a picture of the riot at Central High in Little Rock, Arkansas, accompanied by the following text:

> Milwaukee's dusky Hank Aaron blasted the Braves into the World Series only a few hours after an insane mob of white supremacists took the Stars and Stripes in Little Rock and tramped it on the ground in front of Central High School.... The cheers that are lifted to Negro ballplayers only dramatize the stupidity of the jeers that are directed at those few Negro kids trying to get a good education for themselves in Little Rock.[17]

From the outset, newspaper coverage of the developing story in Little Rock and the Braves drive for the National League flag ran concurrently through the first three weeks of September. On September 23, the pennant race and race relations collided head on.

Aaron may not have been aware of the battle being waged by Thurgood Marshal and others in Arkansas during the heated final weeks of the baseball season. But by the time President Dwight Eisenhower sent federal troops to escort black students through the halls of Central High, he would have time to consider the situation of the evolving world while he prepared for his first World Series.

The Braves opponent in the Fall Classic would be the third incarnation of the New York Yankees great dynasty teams. The seemingly invincible Yankees had represented the American league in eight of the last ten World Series, winning seven times. With a 98–56 record, the Yankees finished eight games in front of the second place Chicago White Sox. Piloted by manager Casey Stengel, the Yanks had finished in first place in all but one year of his stewardship. The sporting press immediately drew comparisons between the star players of the two teams—Aaron, who led the NL with 44 home runs and 132 RBIs, and Mickey Mantle, who captured the American League's Triple Crown with 52 home runs, 130 RBIs, and a .353 batting average. The Yankees pitching staff boasted five hurlers who won in double figures, including future Hall-of-Famer Whitey Ford, who was well on his way to becoming the winningest pitcher in World Series history. Ford would face Warren Spahn in the first game. The Braves one-two punch of Spahn and Burdette made them formidable foes, although the Yankees were still heavy favorites over the less experienced Milwaukee club, which was tagged with a "Bushville" label for their small-town heritage. However, riding on their late-season momentum, the Braves and their fans approached the Series with a great deal of confidence.

The Series began in New York and provided Aaron with his first glimpse of Yankee Stadium. Game 1 was all Whitey Ford. Aaron got one of the five hits Ford surrendered in a 3–1 complete game victory. Lew Burdette matched Ford's effort the next day, with a complete game of his own while Aaron tripled and scored as the Braves salvaged a split of the first two games in New York.

The Series returned to Milwaukee for the first World Series game ever played in the city. The Yankees once again gained the upper hand administering a 12–3 drubbing behind pitcher Don Larsen, who came on early in relief of Bob Turley. Aaron was the only hitter who posed a threat to Larsen, connecting for his first home run of the Series, a two-run blast in the fifth inning.

Spahn brought the Braves back, pitching all ten innings of a dramatic fourth game. The Yankees rallied for three runs in the ninth to tie the score at 7–7 and force extra innings; a shoe polished scuffed ball kept the Braves hopes alive as they battled back in the tenth. Pinch hitter Vernal "Nippy" Jones batted for Spahn to lead off the Braves half of the tenth. The first pitch was a low ball in the dirt that Jones believed hit him in the foot and he began walking towards first base. Umpire Augie Donatelli did not acknowledge that the ball had hit Jones and an argument between the two ensued. The ball had bounced off the retaining wall behind home plate and Jones picked it up and presented it to Donatelli pointing out where the polish from his shoe had left a scuff on the ball. Donatelli awarded Jones first base. Felix Mantilla came in as a pinch runner for Jones. Red Schoendienst bunted Mantilla over to second and Johnny Logan singled him home with the tying run. Eddie Mathews followed with the decisive blow, a game-ending two-run blast. Aaron hit his second home run of the Series, singled, and drove in 3 runs in the Braves win. Burdette continued to foil the Yankees, scattering 7 hits over 9 shutout innings in Game 5 while Aaron remained hot, going 2 for 3 in a 1–0 win.

The Series returned to New York for Game 6. Aaron and Frank Torre hit solo home runs off Bob Turley, who gave up only two other hits while going the distance for a 3–2 Yankees win that once again evened the Series. In Game 7, Burdette extended his string of shutout innings pitched to 24 with his third straight complete-game victory, earning the Braves their first World Series championship and a Series MVP award for himself with a seven-hit 5–0 gem. Aaron collected two more hits and drove in the game's first run. He went on to lead all Series hitters with a .393 average, three home runs, and seven RBIs. Aaron was named the National Leagues' MVP a few weeks later edging batting champion Stan Musial of the Cardinals and teammate Red Schoendienst in a closely contested vote for the award. It was a fitting finale to what would prove to be the most fondly recalled season of his career. "All of those things made 1957 the best year of my baseball life, and it went along with the best year of baseball that any city ever had. It doesn't get any better than Milwaukee in 1957," said Aaron.[18]

NOTES

1. Aaron, with Bisher, *Aaron*, 76.
2. Ibid.
3. Musick, *Hank Aaron*, 82.
4. Aaron, with Wheeler, *I Had a Hammer*, 126.
5. Musick, *Hank Aaron*, 84.
6. Aaron, with Bisher, *Aaron*, 81.
7. Ibid.
8. Ibid., 83.
9. Ibid., 83.
10. Ibid., 84.
11. Ibid., 93.
12. Aaron, with Wheeler, *I Had a Hammer*, 99.
13. Ibid., 100.

14. Aaron, with Bisher, *Aaron*, 96.
15. Ibid.
16. Aaron, with Wheeler, *I Had a Hammer*, 126.
17. Ibid.
18. Ibid., 130.

THE END OF TWO ERAS,
1958–1966

While the Braves drive for the pennant and World Series victory put Aaron at the center of the baseball universe in 1957, the big story lurking in the background was the impending move to the West Coast of the Brooklyn Dodgers and New York Giants. Citing "cramped" conditions at Ebbets Field, including a lack of adequate parking space, Dodgers owner Walter O'Malley had been threatening to pack his team up since the beginning of the 1956 season. Giants owner Horace Stoneham was also seeking a new ballpark deal in Manhattan and when the plan for a proposed 110,000-seat stadium was nixed he entertained the idea of joining O'Malley out west. On May 29, 1957, the National League approved the relocation of the Dodgers and Giants to the West Coast if the clubs formally declared their intentions to move. The Giants were the first to make it official when the team's board of directors voted in favor of the move on August 19. The Dodgers announcement came on October 8, an off-day between Games 5 and 6 of the 1957 World Series.

The relative success of the Braves move to Milwaukee served as an impetus, instigating and propelling the Dodgers and Giants westward leanings. If the Braves could draw more than two million fans in Milwaukee, how many fans would come out to see storied franchises like the Giants and Dodgers in the thriving new metropolises in California?

The new frontier was waiting. In the years to follow, both the National and American Leagues would grow in response to the American population's westward migration. Little did Aaron realize at the time that the moving of the Dodgers and Giants to California and the expansion of both leagues would

Aaron is greeted by Dusty Baker after hitting home run number 703 off Expos pitcher Steve Renko in Montreal on August 17, 1973. *National Baseball Hall of Fame Library, Cooperstown, N.Y.*

spread major league baseball in all directions, and that the Milwaukee Braves would themselves eventually pack up and head to previously uncharted terrain. But there was still some quality time to be spent in Milwaukee and the Braves had at least one more glory year in them.

In the winter of 1957–1958, Barbara Aaron gave birth prematurely to a pair of twin boys, Larry and Gary. Gary died without ever leaving the hospital and the first few months of Larry's life were very uncertain. The family journeyed to Mobile, where Aaron's mother Estella cared for Larry and most likely saved his life. In Mobile, Henry Aaron was given a day named in his honor. It seemed a long way for him to come in such a short time and he suspected he was the first black person ever given a key to the city. Just when it seemed there were no limits to his old city's newfound kindness, Aaron found where the line was drawn. Asked to a be the guest speaker at a luncheon for one of Mobile's civic organizations, Aaron asked if he could bring Barbara, to which the group responded that it was a stag affair. Aaron asked if he could then bring his father? When again the response was no, Aaron declined the invitation. He was not sure if he was the reason, but while Aaron was still in town the local KKK held a cross burning.

In Wisconsin during the final weeks of the off-season, Aaron, despite his World Series hero stature, was once again subject to both subtle and overt forms of racism in his new hometown of Mequon. These acts included a neighbor apologizing for his dog growling with an off-handed disclaimer of how unfamiliar the pooch was with "colored people," and a series of obscene phone calls made to women in the neighborhood by an anonymous caller falsely identifying himself as Aaron.

Hank was now a 23-year-old father of three. Hankie Jr., the couple's first son, was born just nine months before Larry and Gary. Estella helped look after all the children during the baseball season and the family spent a lot of time traveling between Mobile and Milwaukee during the off-season. About this same time, Aaron made the acquaintance of Father Mike Sablica, a Milwaukee Catholic priest interested in the Civil Rights movement, who saw in Aaron a high profile personality who could assist in advancing that cause. Sablica was quoted as follows in the Aaron authobiography *I Had a Hammer*:

> At the time, Hank was aware of social problems, but he was not articulating this awareness. He expressed himself to me, but he didn't do it publicly because he didn't want to be known as a troublemaker. I thought it would be beneficial for him to become a Catholic. In those days, I had a lot of black converts at my church, St. Boniface. I would naively tell them that the Catholic Church was their only hope to get their civil rights.[1]

Aaron, Barbara, and Gaile were all baptized at the Catholic Church in Milwaukee.

On their final trip south before spring training in 1958, the Aarons stopped in Jacksonville to visit Barbara's family. Hank met up with teammate Felix Mantilla, who rode in Aaron's new Chevrolet Malibu to the Braves camp in Bradenton, Florida. Along the way, a couple of white kids in a Buick ran Aaron's car off the road. Bouncing through a ditch before steering the car back onto the road and avoiding collisions with oncoming traffic, Aaron and Mantilla narrowly escaped injury.

When Aaron arrived in Bradenton, he told some of his teammates what happened and was told to avoid mentioning it to reporters lest they call the NAACP. "I almost lost my life," Aaron replied, "and you want me to keep it a secret?"[2] The incident served as an impetus for Aaron to begin speaking up on race-related issues. Bolstered by his increasing stature, the usually quiet Aaron began to find his voice, and this time he could not hold his tongue. He used the regular question-and-answer sessions with reporters to relate the story of his highway mishap and to file further grievances on other race-related issues.

In a 1958 *New York Times* magazine article entitled "The Panther at the Plate," writer William Furlong included a boxed sidebar with the subhead "Race Relations."

> One subject on which Aaron feels deeply and toward which he displays no indolence is race relations. Last summer he bought a four-bedroom house in a middle class white neighborhood in Milwaukee. There have been no stonings or cross burnings. Instead, the neighborhood kids lie in wait to ask, "How should I hold my bat, Henry?" or "How do you catch the high ones, Henry?"
>
> "I don't know how he stands it," says one of his neighbors. "He's got more patience than any man I've ever seen."
>
> "My neighbors are real nice, warm friendly folks," says Aaron. "I couldn't have picked a nicer place to live." But he doesn't kid himself about his position in the neighborhood. "I don't think the average colored person could live there," he says, "They accept me because I'm a baseball player, but I just want to get along with them because I'm a human being. All I want is what most people want—a decent place for my wife and kids. It doesn't make no difference if people don't want to talk to me."[3]

Aaron was generally, if gradually, respected and carved out a niche for himself in Milwaukee.

Back on the ballfield, the Braves were experiencing a new kind of scrutiny. Any championship team knows the pressure of having to do it again. Although the Braves did make it to the top of the National League for the second consecutive season in 1958 it was hard to muster the same magic from the year before.

Last year's pennant race hero, Hurricane Hazle blew out of town on May 24, traded to Detroit after batting just .179 in 20 games and was practically never heard from again. His brief career was relegated to footnote status; he hit .241 in 43 games for the Tigers, giving him a composite average of .211 with 2 home runs and 10 RBIs for the season. Flashing through like a comet, Hurricane hit .311 in small parts of three separate seasons with nine home runs, 37 RBIs, 37 runs scored, one incredibly memorable summer in Milwaukee, and a big fat World Series ring on his finger.

After struggling early in the season, the Braves still managed to breeze to the pennant, finishing eight games in front of second-place Pittsburgh, this time without the dramatics of an eleven-inning home run. Aaron did contribute a seventh-inning blast against the Cincinnati Reds, whom the Braves trailed 5–4 at the time, in the clincher on September 21.

Aaron's home-run production fell from 44 in 1957 to 30 in 1958 and he was beat out by Mathews' 31 for the team lead. He also drove in 37 fewer runs with 95, but still led the team, while raising his average four points to .326. Warren Spahn tied for the league lead with 22 victories, followed close behind by Burdette's 20. Once again, the Braves met the Yankees, who had just about the same team, in the Series. Behind Spahn and Burdette the Braves took a commanding three-games-to-one lead. The Yankees gained a measure of revenge on their prior Series nemesis, tagging Burdette for losses in Games 5 and 7. Aaron compiled 9 more hits, giving him a total of 20 with a .364 average for the two World Series that he imagined would be just the beginning of a lengthy October resume. However in the 18 subsequent years of his playing career, he would never participate in another Fall Classic.

The disappointing conclusion to the Series marked the beginning of the end for the Braves in Milwaukee. The team fought tooth and nail with the Dodgers again in 1959, with the regular season ending in a dead heat that forced a three-game playoff, but the Braves succumbed with two quick losses and finished out of the money. For his part, Aaron had another great season knocking 39 long balls with 123 RBIs and a league leading .355 average. Once again, Mathews beat him out with a team-high and league-leading 46 home runs. Overall, the Braves performance can best be described as lackluster and manager Fred Haney caught the wrath of new Braves executive vice president Birdie Tebbetts, who earned his reputation as a hot-headed, mean-spirited bench jockey in his days as manager of the Cincinnati Reds. In Aaron's opinion, the Braves had become complacent and the signs were visible as early as spring training. As Aaron remembered it, Haney let out his frustration in a closed door lambasting in Bradenton.

> I don't know if you guys came to Florida this spring to be playboys or ballplayers. You've won two pennants in a row. You've been in two World Series in a row. You've carried home some pretty fat paychecks. You've also started carrying some pretty fat asses. What's wrong, don't you like the big leagues? Don't you like the Braves? Don't you like yourselves? Well if you don't, keep it up the way you're going and about half of you are going to wind up in Wichita.[4]

At season's end, Haney turned in his resignation during the middle of the World Series played between the Dodgers and the Chicago White Sox. Chuck Dressen replaced Haney and managed the Braves to yet another second-place finish, but in Aaron's summation failed to connect with many of his players. "Here's a guy who has more baseball knowledge than any manager I've played for. But I personally think when he came to our club he handled things wrong. He tried to make Spahn and Burdette do things they weren't capable of and they resented it," said Aaron.[5]

The Braves finished seven games behind frontrunning Pittsburgh and were slipping into an era of mediocrity that would plague the club for almost an entire decade. Aaron was his usual consistent self with a league-leading 126 RBIs. He also hit .292 with 40 home runs, connecting for his 200th career blast on July 3 and finishing the season with 219 over the course of his seven big league seasons.

In the off-season, a big story broken by sportswriter Wendell Smith of the *Chicago American* concerning the living conditions of black players during spring training in Florida was front-page news. On January 23, 1961, under the headline "Negro Ball Players Want Rights in South," Smith wrote:

> Beneath the apparently tranquil surface of baseball there is a growing feeling of resentment among Negro Major leaguers who still experience embarrassment, humiliation, and even indignities during spring training in the south.
>
> The Negro player who is accepted as a first class citizen in the regular season is tired of being a second class citizen in spring training.[6]

Smith's story was the first in a series of articles chronicling the experiences of black players working and training alongside white teammates on the ballfield while being almost completely segregated in all other aspects of life.

> The Negro player resents the fact that he is not permitted to stay in the same hotels with his teammates during spring training, and is protesting the fact that he cannot eat in the same restaurants, not enjoy other privileges.
>
> At the moment he is not belligerent. He is merely seeking help and sympathy and understanding, and a solution.[7]

Smith called for major league team owners to "exert their influence," in the form of boycotting segregated hotels in Florida, citing the impact spring training exhibition games and related activities had on the local economy.

Aaron was quoted in another piece written by Smith one week later, appearing in the *American* on February 6, one day after Aaron's 27th birthday. In response to a comment made by Tebbets, who claimed that the Negro members of the club are "satisfied with their spring training housing arrangement," Aaron said the executive vice president of the Braves was wrong. Describing the accommodations for Negro Players at Bradenton, Florida, Aaron declared, "There is really only room for 4 men, and last year there were 8 or 10 living there. Beds have to be put in the hall and if players don't hustle to the bathroom in the morning, the last man up doesn't get any hot water."[8] Aaron was referring to the house of Mrs. Lulu Gibson, where he and the Braves other black players had lived during every spring training season he had been with the team.

A few weeks later, Smith wrote a story about a white Sarasota, Florida husband and wife who rented hotel rooms to eight black members of the Chicago White Sox against open and hostile local opposition. "The Wachtels, bitterly opposed to any form of segregation or discrimination, volunteered to take in rejected players. They are paying a heavy social penalty and taking a daring risk for their benevolent stand against the deep-rooted bigotry, which exists in this southern town of 45,000 people."

In the same article, Edward Wachtel described some of the threats and harassment he received from the community.

> When it was first discovered that I was going to accept these players, people called us all hours of the day and night and demanded that I refuse them.
>
> They warned that if I didn't, they would bomb us out. We received calls from men who said they were members of the Ku Klux

Klan and that they were going to burn a fiery cross on my front lawn.[9]

Smith continued his newspaper campaign to desegregate all major league spring training camps throughout the course of the 1961 season, and Major League Players' Association (MLPA) representative Judge Robert Cannon said the issue would be on the agenda at the association's annual meeting in Boston on August 1.

Aaron again voiced his opinion in the *American* on the eve of the association meetings. "I'm sick and tired of being shoved into rooming houses and forced to eat in second class restaurants. If I'm a big leaguer, I want to live like one," said Aaron.[10]

Wendell Smith wrote, "It is impossible for anyone, unless he has actually experienced it, to visualize what it is like to be a Negro baseball player in Florida during the spring season. To the average white player, the six weeks spent here training is merely a blink of a pleasant time in a ballplayer's life, but to his Negro teammate it is an eternity of humiliations and frustrations."[11]

In 1960, Joe Torre got into two games with the big league club as a pinch hitter, singling in two at-bats. A year later, he was the Braves starting catcher and by 1964 he was firmly entrenched in the batting order, earning an All-Star spot and finishing the season with a .321 average, 20 home runs, and 109 RBIs. As a 21-year-old rookie with the Braves in 1961, Torre did not realize the separate treatment Aaron and the Braves other black players were receiving during spring training.

"Unfortunately I never was aware of racial problems because I wasn't segregated and I was immature and young. Not that it didn't make a difference but when I went through high school it wasn't a part of my life. I had blacks in my class, friends and all that stuff," recalled Torre of his Brooklyn, New York, childhood. "I found out later, after talking to Bob Gibson about what he had to go through as a minor leaguer, and a big leaguer in spring training and all those things. It made me sick to my stomach it really did," said Torre.[12]

Thinking back, Torre recalled the differences between his first two springs with the club.

> I guess it was in 1961 or 1962, in spring training one year we were staying at the Bradenton Cabana, which was a new hotel in Bradenton. The following year we moved to the Twilight Motel because the Braves organization had decided we were not going to be segregated any more. We moved everybody into the motel so we could all stay under the same roof and eat under the same roof because we had a private dining room.

That was the first real awareness I had that it was a major problem even for baseball players. It was great that we did that in retrospect. I was very proud to be a part of that movement. It had to be
very tough when you consider what they had to endure, what Jackie
Robinson had to endure in 1947, and it's basically your culture, it's
the way people were brought up—that's why so many players gave
him such a hard time.[13]

When Aaron and the other black Braves were finally allowed access to the
team hotel in 1962, at least one person was upset by the change—Mrs. Lulu
Gibson, whose home the black players had resided in each spring. Aaron later
recalled the following exchange with Mrs. Gibson:

I ran into Mrs. Gibson on the street a few weeks later, and she was
crushed. She figured I was behind the move—I suppose I was—and
it made her feel as if I'd walked out on her. She said, "Don't you love
me? Don't you like being in our home?" I said, "Mrs. Gibson, that's
not it at all. I love your home, but it's time now for baseball to understand that we have to have a choice of where we want to stay, and
you have to understand that too. It's very important that we make
that statement." But Mrs. Gibson didn't see it that way. She said, "I
don't think you like us anymore." That was the last time I saw her.[14]

Despite the progress the Braves had made regarding race relations, equal treatment for all, and a harmonious clubhouse atmosphere, the team continued to
crumble on the field throughout the early 1960s. The players did not respond
well to Charlie Dressen's old school technique, although the Braves remained in
the hunt for most of the 1961 season. Despite posting a record of 83–71,
Dressen was fired with twenty-five games left in the season and replaced by
Birdie Tebbetts. Under Tebbetts, the Braves went 12–13 down the stretch, finishing in fourth place, ten games behind frontrunning Cincinnati. Aaron played
in every game of the season, knocking 34 homers, with 120 RBIs and a .327
average.

Prior to the 1961 season, a new pair of middle infielders, shortstop Roy
McMillan and second baseman Frank Bolling, were acquired at the cost of young
pitchers Joey Jay and Juan Pizarro, and the fan favorite Bill Bruton. The trade
changed the team's dynamic and clubhouse atmosphere. Joey Jay went on to
lead the National League with 21 victories for the league champion Cincinnati
Reds, and Pizarro went 14–7 with a 3.05 ERA for the AL's Chicago White Sox.

The love affair between the fans and the team had lost its luster and it was
clear the honeymoon was over. New policy dictating that Braves fans could no

longer bring their own coolers full of beer contributed to the city's rapidly increasing indifference towards the team. "Those people in Milwaukee had been accustomed for years to coming to the ballpark toting their own buckets full of beer, and this seemed to them like they were being denied a constitutional right, or something like that," recalled Aaron.[15] Attendance figures had been slowly ebbing from the lofty heights of the record-breaking 2.2 million in the championship season of 1957. In 1962, the figures dropped dramatically, from more than 1.1 million in the previous year to 766,921.

Despite one of Aaron's best seasons, with 45 home runs, 128 RBIs, and a .323 average, the Braves fell to fifth place in 1962. Aaron's most memorable moment of the season was a 470-foot blast, the longest ball he ever hit. The monster home run came at the Polo Grounds in New York off Jay Hook of the expansion New York Mets. It was only the third or fourth ball in history to reach the center-field bleachers of the old stadium; Babe Ruth hit one in the 1920s before the bleacher seating was moved back. Aaron's teammate Joe Adcock was the first to do it after the move, and amazingly enough a skinny young Chicago outfielder named Lou Brock had hit one to the right-field side of Aaron's shot just the night before. Aaron was rewarded for his efforts in 1962 with a hike in pay putting his salary at about $50,000.

The team's slide continued in 1963, as the Braves slipped to sixth. Aaron, however, maintained his personal level of excellence, leading the league with 44 home runs and 130 RBIs. Biographer Phil Musick wrote the following of Aaron's consistency during the Braves lean years: "And as they crumbled, he stood shock still in the ruins, something of excellence to which the rapidly disillusioned Milwaukee fans could cling."[16]

Aaron hit the 300th homer of his career on April 19, 1963, off the Mets Roger Craig in New York. Given the green light by new manager Bobby Bragan, Aaron finished second in the National League with 31 stolen bases in 36 attempts. As manager, Bragan was a welcome change from Tebbetts. Bragan responded to rumors that the Mets were interested in purchasing Aaron's contract for half-a-million dollars by giving Aaron votes of confidence on all levels; Bragan said he wouldn't trade Hank for a million.

By this time Aaron was among the most seasoned veterans on the club and was looked to and regarded by the younger players and new members of the team as a leader. Lou Klimchock, a utility infielder, who played for four teams in his twelve-year career and later became president of the Arizona chapter of the Major League Baseball Players Alumni Association (MLBPAA), was 23 when he joined the Braves in 1962. Klimchock recalled that "[Aaron] had that presence where you could see the greatness. My first spring training, he came in a little late with an injury, his first game he came in as a pinch hitter, hit a home run, walks off a plane and hits a home run in his first at bat. Guys would gather around him when he was talking because he didn't talk that much."[17]

Lou Klimchock played with the Braves for parts of four seasons from 1962 to 1965, until the end of the team's run in Milwaukee. He got into 10 games in 1964, notching 7 hits in 21 at-bats for a .333 average, with 2 RBIs and 3 runs scored. Five years later, supporting the theory that what a player really needs is an opportunity to play, Klimchock hit .287 with 6 home runs and 23 RBIs while splitting time between third and second base in 90 games for the Cleveland Indians. Klimchock recalled Aaron as the best player of his era.

> Seeing him on a day to day basis, I always thought Hank was a better ballplayer than Willie Mays or Frank Robinson. If he saw an outfielder hesitate for an instant he would go from first to third on a single and be there, standing up, so far ahead of the throw. When you see a guy everyday you see the little things that make him a better ballplayer. Hank didn't get the notoriety playing in a small market.[18]

One Aaron anecdote that stood out in Klimchock's memory involved an event that occurred outside a regular game situation. "We were in Philly in 64, when they faded, prior to one of the games in that series there was an impromptu home run hitting contest during batting practice before the game. He hit the first 8 or 10, 11, 12, pitches he was thrown out the park off our batting practice pitcher Ken Silvestri. People started noticing and began to keep a count. It got up to 23 in a row!"[19]

Klimchock recalled Aaron as a player who recognized and accepted young players who were on their way up: "He never big leagued you. He knew the young guys would eventually have to take over and he really helped those guys. On the side he would counsel guys. He might explain how he would handle a certain situation or what he would do if he were at bat, and we would think 'well that's you, we're not that good.'"[20]

Although their conversations were infrequent, Klimchock had a slight edge over some of the other youngsters when approaching Aaron. "I was very fortunate because I played with Tommie and through that association that made me O.K. with him," said Klimchock.[21]

By the time Aaron's younger brother Tommie cracked the Braves major league roster in 1962 after toiling in the minors for four years, big brother Hank had hit 253 big league home runs. Following six years behind his brother's footsteps, Tommie played for the same Eau Claire club in 1958 and 1959 that Hank did. Seven years after Hank, Garner, and Mantilla had integrated the South Atlantic League, Tommie began the 1960 season in Jacksonville before moving to Cedar Rapids and Louisville. Tommie hit .299 for Austin in 1961, which contributed to his making the Braves roster as a 22-year-old major league rookie in 1962. He immediately began drawing inevitable comparisons to his brother, which he would endure for the duration of his professional career.

Hank Aaron's brother-in-law, Bill Lucas, who would later become baseball's highest-ranking African American, first as the Braves director of minor league operations, and later as director of player personnel, said it was almost impossible for Tommie to receive an objective analysis. "I've always said that if his name had been Tommie Jones instead of Tommie Aaron he would have gotten a better shot," Lucas was quoted as saying in a 1973 *Sport* magazine article. "At Austin once I remember he hit a long home run and as he was circling the bases some fan yelled, 'Hey Tommie, Hank hit two today.' It was always like that."[22]

During his rookie season of 1962, Tommie hit 8 home runs for the Braves in 141 games, with 38 RBIs and a .231 batting average, playing predominantly at first base. Three times during the 1962 season both Aarons homered in the same game. Struggling under high expectations, Tommie played sporadically through parts of six more seasons while never fully realizing the potential many had predicted for him. He hit 5 more home runs over the course of his final six major league seasons raising his career total to 13, placing him with Hank at the top of the list for home runs hit by big league brothers. The 768 home runs Tommie and Hank compiled collectively by the end of their careers outdistanced the three DiMaggio—Joe, Vince, and Dom—who collectively hit 573.

Although Tommie was at times disheartened by his relationship with the Braves organization as a player, he handled his relative stature to his brother with aplomb. "Hell, not everyone can be Hank Aaron. That guy is unique in the world," said Tommie.[23]

Bouncing back and forth from the majors to the minors in the mid-1960s, Tommie enjoyed his finest season as a professional in 1967, hitting .309 with 11 home runs and 56 RBIs and earning the International League MVP award playing for the Richmond Braves pennant-winning team. In 1972, the season after his final major league stint, Tommie became a player-coach for the Richmond minor league club and took over as manager. Because of Tommie and Hank's age difference and the distance between them when Hank became a major leaguer, the Aaron brothers did not have a very close relationship until later in life. In 1982, just five years after becoming a manager, Tommie was diagnosed with leukemia. He died in 1984.

The brief period during which Tommie and Hank were teammates coincided with an era of dominance for black players in the National League that made Hank wonder about the caliber of major league baseball talent before black players had arrived. Conversely, Aaron also considered what the quality of Negro League baseball had been when the two races were still separated.

When baseball Commissioner Ford Frick was asked for his assessment of baseball in the time since integration, he delivered remarks that confounded Aaron. Said Frick:

> Baseball evolved in slavery days. Colored people did not have a chance to play it then, and so were late in developing proficiency. It was more than fifty years after the introduction of baseball before colored people in the United States had a chance to play it. Consequently, it was another fifty years before they by natural process, arrived at the stage where they were important in the organized baseball picture. And as quickly as they attained that importance, organized baseball began to show an interest in them.[24]

"What I don't understand," said Aaron "is, if it took us fifty years to pick up a bat and another fifty years to learn how to swing it, by what miracle did we come to dominate the National League after only ten or fifteen more? The way I saw it, the commissioner's remarks were an insult to Satchel Paige and Josh Gibson and every black player who came before Jackie."[25]

While baseball was always at the forefront of Aaron's consciousness, it was at about this time that a rising social awareness had also begun to occupy his mind. That same summer in Birmingham in Aaron's home Alabama state, under the direction of Sheriff Bull Connor, firemen opened up high powered hose nozzles to blast civil rights protestors off the streets and sidewalks. In August 1963, Dr. Martin Luther King Jr. delivered his "I Have a Dream" speech in Washington D.C., and two weeks later in Birmingham, a bomb exploded at the Sixteenth Street Baptist Church killing four little girls attending a Sunday school class.

Aaron hit a home run in St. Louis that day. He continued to make his contribution to society on the ballfield, one of the few places in America where blacks and whites worked alongside each other. And when and where he could, Aaron became involved in the Civil Rights movement by reading the writings of authors like James Baldwin and using his public voice to endorse political candidates.

Aaron has often been characterized as a quiet player who "kept his commitment to the civil rights movement out of the headlines."[26] This image of Aaron was crafted early on when he began his professional career as a relatively shy teenager and was perpetuated throughout his playing days. Perhaps he was not afforded as many opportunities or forums as other athletes, politicians, or public figures, or maybe it just wasn't reported when he did speak out. But there is certainly ample evidence to support the contrary notion that Aaron was indeed a vocal proponent of equal rights and due justice for African Americans on and off the field during the early years of the Civil Rights movement.

Aaron was quoted as follows in the August 1964 issue of *Sport* magazine, which excerpted his words from the book *Baseball Has Done It*:

> I've read some of James Baldwin's books. He is a very good author with very good ideas . . . Baldwin says we've waited long enough. If you wait long enough you can break anything down. We'll we've been waiting all this time, my parents are waiting right now in Alabama. The whites told my parents, "Wait and things'll get better." They told me, "Wait and things'll get better." They're telling these school kids, "Wait and it'll be better." Well, we're not going to wait any longer! We're doing something about it. That's what Baldwin says. He's right.[27]

As he did a few years earlier concerning the living conditions during spring training in Florida, Aaron was continuing to be recognized as a player who was not apprehensive about speaking up and confronting injustice. In this, Aaron surprised some of his contemporaries, other black players who were still holding their tongues.

With Chicago sportswriter Jerome Holtzman, Aaron wrote an article for *Sport* magazine under the headline "Are You Ready for a Negro Manager? I Could Do the Job." In the article, Aaron wrote:

> I've been thinking about this for a month now and I've given it good, hard thought and I'm still not certain where to start. But I am convinced I could manage a big-league club and that there are many other Negroes who could also have managerial qualifications—or will have. Willie Mays could manage. So could Jackie Robinson. Bill White could manage and Billy Bruton and Junior Gilliam and Ernie Banks. You don't have to cut this list off. It can go on and on because no two managers manage the same way.[28]

Concerning Aaron's outspokenness, Frank Robinson, who actually became the first black manager in both the American and National Leagues, said: "When Hank was speaking out I said, 'oh my goodness Hank, you've lost it. Have you gone crazy?' I used to shake my head and say 'boy Hank you better be quiet' because in those days baseball executives could bury you. They could bury a black ball player."[29]

After ten big league seasons—the period from 1954 to 1964—in which Aaron led all major leaguers in batting average (.319) and home runs (366), he did not seem to have any fear of being buried. However, the Braves as a team were unable to dig themselves out of the hole they had fallen into early in the 1964 season. Despite winning 20 of the season's final 26 games, the Braves still finished fifth, 5 games behind the St. Louis Cardinals, who surged past a Philadelphia team that had held a 6½-game lead with only 12 left to play. Aaron slumped as well, hitting only 24 home runs compared to 44 the year before. He also drove in 35 fewer runs, although he did hit .328 and was named to his 13th consecutive All Star Game.

Prior to the 1963 season, the Braves had been sold by Lou Perini to a group of Chicago businessmen. As attendance figures in Milwaukee continued to slide, rumblings from the south carried rumors that the team was headed for Atlanta. On October 21, 1964, the Braves board of directors voted to ask the National League for permission to move the team to Atlanta. The request was granted and on November 10 the Braves signed a twenty-five-year lease to play in the yet-to-be built Atlanta Fulton County Stadium.

The deal had been conducted mostly behind closed doors, requiring numerous contingencies before members of the Atlanta business community would pony up in support of a new stadium and team. "We built a stadium on ground we didn't own, with money we didn't have, for a team we hadn't signed," said former Atlanta Mayor Ivan Allen.[30] Allen was a progressive thinker who would be described as a moderate a generation after his term, but he was more of a radical at the time. An early proponent of integration, he was the only white southern politician to testify in support of the Civil Rights Act of 1964.

While the machinations were quietly at work in Atlanta, the city of Milwaukee filed suit and obtained a court injunction that would keep the team in town for another year. "The circumstances of this transfer definitely give big-league baseball a black eye," Milwaukee Mayor Henry Maier told newspaper reporters.[31] It would in effect be a lame duck season for the Braves, whose fans knew the team was living on borrowed time. "This is a sad day for baseball," said Wisconsin Governor John Reynolds. "The owners of the Braves are showing a callous lack of faith in the people of Milwaukee and Wisconsin."[32]

Aaron didn't necessarily want the team to move either. "I was there nine or 10 years ago and I have no intention of playing under those conditions again," Aaron said. "There's no doubt about it; the South is segregated and I just don't want to play under those conditions."[33] However, the move was inevitable and beyond the control of Aaron, any other players, or the fans.

From the dizzying heights of romance the team and the city of Milwaukee were engaged in for most of the previous decade, the fans in 1965 responded like spurned lovers as attendance dwindled to an all-time low of 555,584. Like Yogi Berra once said, "If people don't want to come to the ballpark, how are you going to stop them?"[34]

The 1965 season saw another fifth-place finish for the Braves and another subpar year for Aaron. His 89 runs batted in were the lowest total he had produced since his rookie season of 1954. His 32 home runs, impressive by anyone else's standards, were a few shy of his average over the past 10 years. He did manage to lead the league with 40 doubles and his .318 average was second best to Roberto Clemente's .329.

On the last day of the season in the last game played by the Braves at County Stadium, Aaron lined into a game-ending double play and the ballpark organist broke into *Auld Lang Syne*. Aaron expressed his feelings on the team's departure to a television reporter: "The thing I will remember the most about Milwaukee and the fans is the way they've opened their hearts up and accepted me and my family into their hearts."[35]

For its part Atlanta welcomed the Braves with open arms. Realizing that the Braves had been an integrated team in a predominantly integrated city, Mayor Allen knew of the apprehension players like Aaron had concerning the team's move to the south. He also knew that easing of racial tension and the integration of the city was essential to economic growth and prosperity. Allen began instituting policies that would cast Atlanta in a new light. He ordered the removal of "white" and "colored" signs from municipal buildings and desegregated public swimming pools, auditoriums, and theaters. At Aaron's own urging, seating in the new ballpark was fully integrated.

Andrew Young, an Atlanta clergyman and high-ranking aide to Martin Luther King Jr., presided over the Southern Christian Leadership Conference in Atlanta. In the mid-1960s, Atlanta had become the center of a black cultural and intellectual renaissance. In April 1966, just prior to the inaugural Opening Day, the city welcomed the Braves with a parade. From his vantage point, Young could see Aaron riding in the back seat of an open convertible and overhead the conversation of two white men. "You know," said one to the other while looking at Aaron, "if we're going to be a big league town he's going to have to be able to live wherever he wants in this town." The meaning of those few words made a lasting impression on their hearer. "I began to realize almost immediately the social impact of Hank Aaron on Atlanta," said Young.[36]

The change the Braves helped bring had an immediate impact on Atlanta and far reaching social ramifications for the entire south. Maynard Jackson, Atlanta's first black mayor, said that as important as baseball was to the development and growth of the South, "there was an issue overriding baseball and that was civil rights."[37]

However, Aaron's appearance on the Atlanta horizon provided the Civil Rights movement with great assistance. According to Andrew Young, he and Martin Luther King Jr. both loved baseball and would occasionally attend Braves games together. "Martin Luther King used to say that it appalled him that eleven o'clock Sunday morning was the most segregated hour of the week, in church, but he was thrilled that by two o'clock in the afternoon, everybody was integrated at the ballpark," said Young.[38]

Congressman John Lewis recalled the juxtaposition of Aaron's accomplishments on the baseball field and the Civil Rights movement in Atlanta: "As he ran the bases a lower segment of America was running with him and he was saying to America 'I want to participate and share in the dream,'" said Lewis.[39]

President Jimmy Carter was a Georgia state senator at the time of the Braves arrival. "It was sports and racially integrated sports teams that brought about the change that saved the South," said Carter. "And I would not have ever been considered seriously as a presidential candidate had that not been done before I ran for office."[40]

NOTES

1. Aaron, with Wheeler, *I Had a Hammer*, 132.
2. Alex Poinsett, "The Hank Aaron Nobody Knows," *Ebony*, July 1974.
3. Furlong, "The Panther at the Plate," 48.
4. Aaron, with Bisher, *Aaron*, 117.
5. Hank Aaron, with Jerome Holtzman, "Are You Ready for a Negro Manager? I Could Do the Job," *Sport* Magazine, October 1965.
6. Wendell Smith, "Negro Ballplayers Want Rights in South," *Chicago American*, January 23, 1961.
7. Ibid.
8. Wendell Smith, "Negro Players Gain in Equality Bid," *Chicago American*, February 6, 1961.
9. Wendell Smith, "Integrates Motel-Periled," *Chicago American*, April 5, 1961.
10. Wendell Smith, "End Spring Degradation, Negro Players Ask," *Chicago American*, July 30, 1961.
11. Wendell Smith, "What a Negro Ballplayer Faces Today in Training," *Chicago American*, April 3, 1961.
12. Author's interview with Joe Torre, September 28, 2003.
13. Ibid.
14. Aaron, with Wheeler, *I Had a Hammer*, 155.
15. Aaron, with Bisher, *Aaron*, 133.
16. Musick, *Hank Aaron*, 93.
17. Author's interview with Lou Klimchock, February 2003.
18. Ibid.
19. Ibid.
20. Ibid.

21. Ibid.

22. Harry Stein, "Tommie Aaron: Only 702 Home runs to go and He'll Break Babe Ruth's Record," *Sport* Magazine, March 1973.

23. Ibid.

24. Harold Seymour, *The People's Game* (Oxford: Oxford University Press, 1990), 533.

25. Aaron, with Wheeler, *I Had a Hammer*, 168.

26. John Holway, *The Sluggers* (Alexandria, VA: Redefintion Books, 1989), 74.

27. Al Stump, "Henry Aaron: Public Image vs. Private Reality," *Sport*, August 1964.

28. Aaron, with Holtzman, "Are You Ready for a Negro Manager? I Could Do the Job."

29. Tollin, *Hank Aaron, Chasing the Dream.*

30. Tolan, *Me and Hank*, 109.

31. Joe Krupinski, "Move to Georgia Peachy? Not to Aaron," *Milwaukee Journal*, October 22, 1964.

32. Ibid.

33. Ibid.

34. Yogi Berra, *The Yogi Book* (New York: Workman Publishing Co., 1998), 36.

35. Tollin, *Hank Aaron, Chasing the Dream.*

36. Tolan, *Me and Hank*, 108.

37. Tollin, *Hank Aaron, Chasing the Dream.*

38. Tolan, *Me and Hank*, 111.

39. Tollin, *Hank Aaron, Chasing the Dream.*

40. Ibid.

THE LAUNCHING PAD,
1966–1972

By the time Aaron left Milwaukee after the 1965 season, he carried a .320 lifetime batting average that placed him highest among active players with five or more years in the majors. His 398 home runs were twelfth on the all-time list and fifth among his contemporaries. Firmly establishing the reputation for consistency that would mark his career, he had hit more than 20 home runs in every season after his rookie year, reaching 30 or more eight times and more than 40 four times for an average of 33 per year.

Having refined his approach at the plate from the free swinging years of his youth, Aaron's hitting style had developed into a sophisticated study of probabilities. Storing information in his brain on pitchers' repertoires and what pitches they were most likely to throw in given situations, Aaron called upon the capacity of his memory in each and every at-bat. Anticipating pitches with such accuracy as if he had known what was coming; to call it "guess hitting" would be selling him short.

"I don't go up there swinging at what they throw me anymore. I've studied and concentrated, and now I wait until I get my pitch," said Aaron to *Sports Illustrated* magazine in August 1966. "He sure as hell does," said Sandy Koufax of the Los Angeles Dodgers. "Did you see him go after that curve I hung for him today? That was a mistake, and you don't get away with a mistake to 'Bad Henry,'" said Koufax, coining a new moniker to go alongside Aaron's "Hammerin' Hank" nickname. "He not only knows what the pitch will be," said Dodgers reliever Ron Perranoski, whom Aaron had beaten to a .812 clip (13 for 16) over the previous six seasons, "but *where* it will be. He's hit one home run

Aaron listening to the voice of Babe Ruth at the National Baseball Hall of Fame in 1974. *National Baseball Hall of Fame Library, Cooperstown, N.Y.*

off me [over the center-field fence at Dodger Stadium] and he went after that pitch as if he'd called for it." "It was a fastball high and away," Aaron recalled. "It was the first pitch, and I guess I was looking for it. I figured he'd try to set me up for the sinker." "Pitchers don't set Henry up," said teammate Gene Oliver. "He sets them up. I honestly believe he intentionally looks bad on a certain pitch just so he'll get it again." "Well not too often," Aaron said. "But say it's a breaking pitch that's going to hit on the plate. I might let my tail fly out a little and miss it and look foolish. Then the pitcher might throw that same pitch for a strike some other time—with two on."[1]

At the All-Star break during his first season in Atlanta, Aaron had already knocked 26 long balls. The move to Atlanta had inspired Aaron to focus more on hitting home runs. Taking full advantage of the highest altitude in the major leagues at the time, combined with high temperatures that held the ball aloft for longer periods of time, Aaron abandoned his line-drive hitting philosophy and began turning on the ball and pulling it more to left field.

He hit his 400th home run off Bo Belinsky in Philadelphia on April 12, 1966, drawing speculation about other milestones, such as when he might reach the 3,000 hit plateau and his eventual place among the game's great sluggers. "That's my goal [3,000 hits]," Aaron told *Sports Illustrated*. "If I make that, I figure things will fall in place." At the time, *Sports Illustrated* writer Jack Mann was among the first to advance the theory of Aaron as a possible breaker of Babe Ruth's career home-run mark.[2]

While Aaron was rediscovering himself as a power hitter, the Braves were suffering through the same mediocrity that plagued them in Milwaukee. The Braves finished in fifth place again with an almost identical record (85–77) to that of the 1965 Milwaukee club (86–76). Aaron finished the 1966 season with a league-leading 44 home runs and 127 RBIs. Although his average dipped to .279, Aaron was more than pleased with his performance at the plate. "I led the league in home runs and RBIs, and this is what I set out to do. There's no better way of making friends when you move into new territory than hitting the ball over the fence. Some people say a guy stealing a base is an exciting thing to watch but there's nothing like a home run to get the fans really excited," said Aaron.[3]

At the conclusion of the 1966 season, Eddie Mathews, Aaron's longest lasting teammate and the Braves most tenured veteran, was traded to the Houston Astros. At 35, Mathews' skills had diminished to a .250 batting average; a career low contribution of 16 home runs, a drop by half from the 32 he hit in 1965; and 53 RBIs, down from 95 the previous year. Still, Aaron did not appreciate the way Mathews was unceremoniously dismissed by the Braves. At the end of their playing days together, Mathews and Aaron had combined for a total of 863 home runs as teammates, surpassing Duke Snider and Gil Hodges (745) for the National League mark and Babe Ruth and Lou Gehrig (793) for the major league record. "Eddie has said that our record is his proudest accomplishment. It makes me proud that he thinks so. I was lucky to have Eddie for a teammate all those years. There's no doubt that he made me a better player," said Aaron.[4]

With Mathews' departure, Aaron became the Braves elder statesman, spiritual leader, and father figure. Nowhere was this more apparent than with young black players during the team's first few years in Atlanta. In 1967, Johnnie B. Baker Jr., more popularly known as "Dusty," was a 17-year-old Braves draft pick out of California's Del Campo High School. At the time, Baker was a scared and uncertain kid. Although a talented multisport athlete, Baker was not sure what to do with his abilities and options. His parents were recently divorced and Baker was living with his mother in the Sacramento suburb of Carmichael.

Baker played nineteen years in the majors, the first eight with the Braves, and another eight with the Dodgers before winding up back in San Francisco and Oakland. He racked up more than 1,900 hits, 242 home runs, and more than 1,000 RBIs with a .278 batting average. He was named to two all-star teams and played in three World Series. Since retiring as a player, he has been wildly successful in his managerial career. Prior to his first season with the Cubs in 2003, he led the San Francisco Giants to either first- or second-place finishes in eight of his ten years at their helm.

Interviewed in the visiting manger's office at Camden Yards in Baltimore in June 2003, Baker stretched out in a comfortable lounge chair and recalled meeting Aaron for the first time.[5] "The Braves were wooing me and kept coming around and finally they took my mom and I to Los Angeles to work out with the team while they were playing at Dodger Stadium." Baker immediately sought out Aaron. "After the work out I asked Hank what would he do if he were me. He said if I had enough confidence in myself that I would be in the big leagues by the time my class was scheduled to graduate college, to go ahead and sign, and if not then go ahead and go to college," said Baker.

Although he was familiar with Aaron as a ballplayer he had followed from a distance; this first meeting with Aaron left a strong and lasting impression on Baker.

> I thought he was one of the strongest most dignified men I'd ever met, physically, spiritually and mentally. He was very, very gracious to my mom and to myself, very humble, you would never have thought that Hank Aaron would be like that, being such a superstar.

You didn't know how superstars were off the field we only knew how they were on the field. It's something I'll always remember.

Baker's mother also spoke with Aaron, asking if he would keep a watchful eye on her son. Baker's memories of Aaron and the life lessons he imparted to a young ballplayer remain vivid and fresh, as if they were delivered yesterday and not 40 years ago.

> I signed with the Braves and went to college in the off season and Hank promised my mother that he would take care of me as if I were his own son. He made me go to church, made me get up in the morning, eat breakfast, made me do all the things that young men really don't like to do. He made me do all the things that you're forced to do at home but you think you're a man when you're away so you don't have to do anymore. I used to hang out on Tenth Street in Atlanta, sometimes down there with the hippies like I did in San Francisco. Hank used to tell me "They don't go for that around here." There's different things that he pulled my coat to about being in the south but at the same time he really didn't like anybody telling him that he shouldn't be in a certain place either. He's a very independent man. He did what he wanted. He said what he wanted. Hank would rarely start a fight or an argument but he certainly wouldn't take anything from anybody either. That's become part of my philosophy as well.
>
> Hank was great to me. He's probably the greatest man I know him and my father. He was like my father away from home. Hank was great as a teammate. When he caught me looking at Willie Mays or Bob Gibson or somebody else and I was gawking at them, he told me "Don't be gawking at them. Respect them but you're going to have to face them. Respect them but don't idolize them. You're in the big leagues."

A pressing concern of both Baker and his mother was the racial climate of the south. "When I got drafted there was only one team I prayed wouldn't draft me and that was the Braves because I didn't want to go to the south. I said "Lord, why?" I didn't think he heard my prayers but evidently I didn't know what his plan was for me and it was the best thing that ever happened to me in my career because of going to the South and meeting Hank Aaron," said Baker.

While Aaron was serving as baseball's first black ambassador to the south, he took younger black players like Baker and later outfielder Ralph Garr under his wing and showed them what their responsibilities were on and off of the field. Baker is aware of the common misconception of Aaron as a quiet man who let his playing do his talking for him and to some extent agrees, but only when it comes to baseball.

> He went about his business quietly on the field but Hank has always spoke up about topics of race. Nobody really listened to him until he broke the record. Then once he broke the record everybody thinks he's supposed to be happy and jolly and forget about different things that happened in his life and inadequacies in society. I used to go to NAACP meetings with him. He was a big supporter of the freedom marches we participated in. I was with him in Atlanta where there were people grabbing at him from all angles. He was big supporter of Operation PUSH with Jesse Jackson when it first got started. Hank's very civic minded and very active.

Born in 1949, two years after Jackie Robinson's breakthrough, Baker arrived almost a generation after Aaron. He grew up on the West Coast and dreamed of being a professional athlete under a different set of circumstances than the ones Aaron had experienced during his childhood in the Deep South.

> People don't realize it but back in those days [Aaron's generation], civil rights and equality were potentially, physically dangerous things to be involved with. People were lynching people, shooting people and throwing them in swamps—all kinds of stuff. My dad and Hank and those guys they come from a different era where they sometimes took more so we wouldn't have to take it later. There's an outer dignity and an inner dignity. Your outer dignity people can penetrate, depending on what the fight is, in order to survive, in order to take care of your family and your household. But that inner dignity is something that he [Aaron] taught me no man should ever tread upon. There's a big "No Trespassing" sign on your inner dignity.

From 1947 to 1967, the year Baker broke in, baseball had been integrated for a full generation. While social advances had been made in baseball and elsewhere in American society, it was by no means a perfect world. "Our generation," said Baker, "was in the process of trying to change some of that via marches, via hippies, via Vietnam, Black Panthers, basic nonconformity as a whole which was probably an aftermath and spillover from what happened in the previous generation. Black Pride. I'm from a generation where we were still Negroes and then somebody called me black and we were ready to fight. We went from Negroes to Blacks to African Americans. Now we're in the African American phase and I find myself still saying Black because that was a sign of my times," said Baker.

Race relations remained a constant theme for America in the 1960s and 1970s. Baker was a teammate of Aaron's during the most tumultuous time of his career—the chase for Babe Ruth's home-run record—a time when receiving hate mail and death threats was part of going to work every day for Aaron. Being around Aaron, helped prepare Baker for some of the scrutiny he would later face as a big league manager. "I used to get a lot of those kind of letters and I tell some of my players the way Hank used to show me and it let me know evidently that I must be getting close to the top because guys on the bottom don't get stuff like that. It let me know that the country hasn't really changed completely," said Baker.

The almost paternal relationship between Aaron and Baker existed across the major league baseball community among black ballplayers of the second and third major league generations. Don Baylor, a 19-year veteran whom, like Baker, went on to become a successful coach and manager, broke in with the Baltimore Orioles in 1970. Baylor crossed paths briefly with Aaron at the end of the latter's career. "I played against him when he was with Milwaukee in the American League," said Baylor during an interview at Turner Field in Atlanta, where he was coaching for the New York Mets in May 2003. "I always respected Hank, Willie Mays, Frank Robinson. I came up under Frank Robinson like Dusty Baker came up under the Hammer so we kind of all had that intertwined relationship for a long time," said Baylor.[6] Willie Mays served in a similar capacity as a mentor for young Bobby Bonds with the San Francisco Giants, developing a relationship that led to Mays becoming godfather to Bonds' son Barry.

"Hank has always been a special person. What Jackie Robinson went through, Hank had to go through during the time when he was trying to break Ruth's record and still concentrate and come out here and do your job every day," said Baylor. "I don't think enough young African American players know the things that Hank and Frank and Jackie Robinson have done for this game."[7]

Aaron expanded his role as an ambassador for baseball on a trip to Vietnam with a small group of baseball stars that included Joe Torre, Harmon Killebrew, Brooks Robinson, Stan Musial, and broadcaster Mel Allen. The trip was designed to boost the morale of U.S. troops. "We didn't sit back at the bases," Aaron told an Associated Press reporter.

We went right to the troops in the field and visited the men in the hospitals. That's what made the trip so good. They were anxious to see us. We created a crowd wherever we went. We talked baseball and showed the movie of last year' All Star Game.

We realized we were in the war zone, but we didn't think we were in any danger. They took every precaution whatsoever. I wasn't afraid. I had never been to the Far East and it was quite an experience to see how the other half lives. You read about Vietnam and how bad off people are, and you think it's a hellhole. But I think it's the most beautiful country I've ever seen.[8]

Orioles third baseman Brooks Robinson was also moved by the three-week long experience. "My lasting impression," Robinson recalled almost forty years later, "was a visit to the hospital. We met young solider who had lost both his legs and here he was apologizing to us for not recognizing Stan Musial."[9]

Back home, Aaron was rewarded for his previous season's efforts with a two-year contract calling for $100,000 annually, a $35,000 hike in pay for each year. While Hank kept hammering away with a league-leading 39 home runs in 1967, bringing his career total to 481, the Braves slid all the way to seventh place with a 77–85 record, the first time the team finished with a losing record since 1952.

In 1968, the Braves rebounded to 81–81, but this time Aaron slumped, hitting 29 home runs with 86 RBIs and a .287 average. However, he connected for his 500th blast off Mike McCormick of the San Francisco Giants at Atlanta on July 14. The Braves and the city of Atlanta recognized his many accomplishments and increasingly significant place in baseball history with a Hank Aaron Day in his honor on August 23.

In 1969, the major league landscape was dramatically altered again with the addition of four new franchises and the separation of the National and American Leagues into Eastern and Western divisions. Oddly enough, the Atlanta Braves were placed in the West with the San Francisco Giants, Los Angeles Dodgers, Houston Astros, Cincinnati Reds, and the expansion San Diego Padres. The East consisted of the New York Mets, Chicago Cubs, Pittsburgh Pirates, St. Louis Cardinals, Philadelphia Phillies, and the expansion Montreal Expos.

The new division format had the desired effect of creating more competitive pennant races; having all twelve teams in the league grouped together had meant that half of them were eliminated before the All-Star break. Aaron's Braves were engaged in a four-team chase for the Western division title with the Giants, Dodgers, and Reds. Aaron led the team's charge, equaling his career single-season high of 44 home runs for the fourth time and driving in 97 runs with an even .300 average. New to the Braves was slugging first baseman Orlando Cepeda, obtained in a trade from St. Louis for Joe Torre. Cepeda knocked 22 home runs with 88 RBIs while hitting behind Aaron in the order. Outfielder Rico Carty hit .348 in 304 at-bats after rebounding from a bout of tuberculosis that had him hospitalized for six months. Knuckleballer Phil Neikro led the Braves pitching staff with 23 wins. The Braves were propelled into first place on a twelfth-inning home run by Aaron against the Dodgers on September 17th, and clinched the NL west flag with their 10th straight win on September 30th.

In the Eastern division, the "Amazin'" New York Mets remained within striking distance of the frontrunning Chicago Cubs throughout the season, eventually taking over first place in mid-September and clinched their divisional pennant before the Braves. The surprising Mets made quick work of the Braves with a three-game sweep in the first National League Championship Series. Despite a self-inflicted hand injury suffered as a result of some late night gallivanting after the Braves pennant clinching victory, Aaron shined in the glare of the hot New York spotlight, hitting home runs in all three games with seven RBIs and a .357 average in the playoff series.

Aaron hit his first playoff home run off Mets pitcher Tom Seaver, the eventual Cy Young Award winner who had led the National League with 25 wins. Seaver, who broke in with the Mets in 1967, said Aaron was his idol as a young aspiring big leaguer. Their first confrontation left a lasting impression on Seaver, who has frequently recounted the story.

> I saw him rise in the on-deck circle, and I had to turn my back. You see, I knew his actions so well—how he'd walk to the plate, rest his bat against his upper right leg, put on his helmet, pick up the bat and step into the box. I couldn't watch that. I didn't want to get emotionally involved in the moment. I was a pro and had to treat him as just another hitter. There was a man on first, I threw a sinker, and Aaron grounded into a double play. "Well," I said to myself, "this league may not be so tough."
>
> Next time up I threw him the same pitch, and he took it into the blue seats far away in that ballpark for a home run. And so my hero taught me a lesson.[10]

At season's end, Aaron had hit 554 career home runs and was earning accolades and recognition from the press concerning his prominent place in the game. In a *Chicago Tribune* story dated September 1, 1969, reporter Robert Markus wrote: "But now Mantle is gone and Mays is slowly grinding to a halt and Aaron swings on, and it is he if anybody, who will challenge Babe Ruth's seemingly unapproachable home run record and it is he too, who will some time next year, join the elite 3,000-hit club. When he reaches it he may quit." At the age of 35, Aaron had begun to ponder the waning days of his career. "I can play now just as well as I ever could. But I can't play as much. I need rest more often now. If I play three or four days in a row, I get tired," said Aaron.[11]

Some of his feelings regarding retirement were spurred by an unlikely source. Braves broadcaster Milo Hamilton had been criticizing the Braves and Aaron in particular despite the team's relatively strong standing during one of Aaron's most productive seasons. The feud between Aaron and Hamilton had its roots in a comment made by Hamilton at a banquet when he introduced Pittsburgh's Roberto Clemente as "a guy you'd have to name to your All-Star team over Hank Aaron." "I love this game," said Aaron, "but I've been in it 16 years and when things like this happen I get to wondering if it's not time to get out. At least out of here. The Braves seem to think more of him than they do of me. I think it's the ball players people come to see, not the radio announcers. They pay him as much as they do me. So if he thinks he can come out and play right field as well as announce, he's welcome to try," said Aaron.[12]

Renowned sports columnist Jim Murray of the *Los Angeles Times* considered Aaron the cream of the crop among his contemporaries and declared him the best right fielder of all time.

> He has right field all to himself for the ages. The Babe will have to move over to the sun field. Henry moved to left field himself for an All-Star game. But he did it because the other outfielders chosen were wary about playing a strange position. The only strange position for Henry Aaron in a ballpark is the bench. The radio announcer who loudly claimed that Henry moved because the other right fielder was better now wishes he had laryngitis that night.[13]

While Aaron was disappointed by what he saw as an underachieving Braves team and its lackluster performance in the playoffs, he appreciated the newfound respect with which he was being treated. Perhaps it was the stage New York provided and his outstanding performance even in defeat or maybe the fact that he was getting on in years and the time left to see him play was growing short.

With determined purpose and a goal of getting back to the playoffs and possibly the World Series, Aaron broke out of the gates in 1970 with one of the most impressive spring training seasons of his career. Aaron collected 21 hits, seven of them home runs, in his first 42 at bats of the Grapefruit League season, averaging a home run in every five trips to the plate.

One month into the season, he reached the inevitable 3,000 hit plateau with a single off Cincinnati's Wayne Simpson. Aaron was the ninth player to reach 3,000 hits and the first to combine 3,000 hits with 500 home runs. Most of the rest of the 3,000-hit club reached the mark two or three generations before, with Stan Musial being the last to accomplish the feat in 1958. Aaron was the first black player to reach 3,000, getting there two months ahead of Willie Mays and thereby drawing attention to the fact that he was also catching up with Mays in home runs. A week later, a feature article on Aaron's accomplishment appeared in the May 23 issue of the *Sporting News*; it made early reference to the type of hate mail Aaron would receive increasingly in years to follow when he drew closer to the home run record. "He files that mail in a special place for keeps and feels sorry for the sender, who of course, never signs his name," wrote Wayne Minshew of the *Sporting News*.[14]

The Braves finished a dismal fifth in 1970, but Aaron had another great year with a .298 average, 118 RBIs, and 38 more home runs, bringing his total to 592. During the off-season, Aaron was divorced from his wife Barbara and moved into an apartment in downtown Atlanta where he began to feel the loneliness and isolation that became of constant companions, as he pursued the home-run record over the next few years. Even though he was regarded not only as one of the game's current luminaries but one of its greatest all-time stars, there were lingering aspects of relative anonymity associated with his public persona.

A *Wall Street Journal* story published on April 5, 1971, referred to Aaron as an "Unsung Slugger" despite the fact that he received more votes for the All Star Game than any player in either league. The story went on to mention that Aaron was almost turned away by the front desk clerk of the hotel in Cincinnati where the game was played when he failed to recognize who Aaron was and painted a familiar picture of Aaron as a soft spoken slugger. Despite his well-chronicled references to racially motivated injustices regarding the place of blacks in baseball throughout the previous fifteen years, the *Journal* article claimed that Aaron had made little attempt to be either a leader of baseball players or a leader of blacks. The article supported this claim with the following quote from Aaron: "I consider myself a baseball player first and a black second and I'm proud of both." The article continued to say that he made it clear he did not want to speak out on either baseball or race. "I have always thought the way I could do the most for my race (and presumably, for his sport) was through excelling in my conduct on and off the field as a player." The story goes on further to claim that according to unnamed friends (sources) in unflattering tone "that he is basically insecure everyplace but on the ball field."[15]

This depiction of Aaron and the use of his own quote contradict numerous previous and future accounts of his speaking up on the topic of race relations in baseball, particularly regarding the lack of consideration given to blacks as managerial candidates and front office employees. In the aforementioned *Sporting News* article of May 1970, less than a year before the *Journal* article was published, Aaron had reiterated sentiments previously expressed in other publications. "I think baseball is running a poor third for the black player," said Aaron. "There is no black major league manager and very few in the front office. Baseball was first a long time ago, but now it runs behind pro football and basketball in their treatment of blacks, especially after our playing days are over."[16]

A year later, when Aaron was asked by *Black Sports* magazine about the advancement of blacks in baseball, he responded quite vocally. "We haven't made any progress at all. The black ballplayer has got to make the owners know about things. If you don't speak out, you don't get anything. I don't think we've said nearly enough, especially the established ballplayer, myself included. As long as I can do things because I'm a ballplayer, then I've got to speak up."[17]

For whatever reasons, a certain portion of the media decided to present its own oversimplified version of Aaron. One indisputable truth was Aaron's place in the racial integration of Atlanta no matter how it was interpreted. Ivan Allen Jr. was Atlanta's mayor when Aaron and the Braves arrived in 1966 and he recalled the almost immediate impact Aaron's presence.

> There was a lot of subtle apprehension about how the South's first major league sports franchise and its black players would go over. Hank played a major role in smoothing the transition and confirming the end of segregation in the South through his thoughtful consideration and cooperative attitude with everyone and his exemplary conduct. He taught us how to do it. The first time he knocked one over that left-field fence, everyone forgot what his color was.[18]

Given the context of Allen's statement, it would appear the former mayor's sentiments were intended to be complimentary, but acceptance of Aaron's color might have been favorable to forgetting his color. At home in the Atlanta neighborhood where he chose to live, his color was well recognized by white neighbors who reportedly moved elsewhere after his arrival.

As the 1971 season approached, speculation of his imminent assault on Ruth's home-run record increased. Statisticians and mathematicians deduced the average number of home runs it would take in the limited amount of time they estimated he had left as a player and prognosticated as to when he would eventually surpass Ruth. Most of the experts figured he would reach 714 some time before the end of the 1974 season.

Aaron reached 600 on April 27, 1971. He hit the blast off San Francisco's Gaylord Perry, which was particularly gratifying because Aaron had always held Perry in disdain for his use of the illegal spit-ball pitch.

In his 1971 All-Star appearance, Aaron finally connected for his first home run in the midsummer classic, an upper-deck blast at Detroit's Tiger Stadium off Oakland A's pitcher Vida Blue. The hit snapped a career-long All Star Game slump for Aaron who had a .175 batting average (10 for 57) in his previous 19 All-Star appearances (two games per season were played from 1959 to 1961) with no extra-base hits.

Aaron continued at an accelerated pace through the second half of the season, blasting a career-high 47 long balls in just 495 at-bats with 118 RBIs and a .327 average, his highest in 10 years. The Braves finished in third place with an 82–80 record. When the 1971 season came to a close, Aaron had 639 home runs, just 75 behind the Babe, and Hank was showing no signs of slowing at age 37. By 1972, it was more a matter of when than whether he would break the record.

Recognition came from more than the press and the fans during the off-season Aaron signed a two-year contract renewal with the Braves, making him the first player to be paid $200,000 annually. The most lucrative contract in baseball history also carried with it heightened expectations and increased scrutiny. As much as Aaron had become a favorite of the Atlanta fans over the previous six seasons, he sensed that a certain portion of the local faithful resented him for his salary combined, possibly, with his race. "As hard as it is for some fans to accept the fact that a ballplayer can make more money than they will earn in a lifetime, they find it repulsive that a black player who maybe never even went to college can be so rich. The Atlanta fans weren't shy about letting me know what they thought of a $200,000 nigger striking out with men on base," said Aaron.[19]

Aaron wasn't shy about justifying his salary either. In the May-June 1972 issue of *Black Sports* magazine Aaron discussed the relative contracts of some of baseball's most well known players.

> But look at Yastrzemski and Mays. Yastrzemski is getting about $170,000 and Mays about $160,000. Who is the better drawing card around the leagues? Who has the best record over the past 10 years? If anyone is worth $200,000, it's Mays. I think I'm worth more than I'm paid. Yastrzemski is white, and Mays is Black. That's the difference. If I were white, I would be making twice as much as I'm making now.[20]

Unfortunately, Aaron followed his spectacular 1971 season with one of the worst years of his career in 1972. The season started with a week-long strike by the players and the Braves suffered through another losing season, finishing fourth in the NL West with a 70-84 record under new manager Eddie Mathews, Aaron's old friend and teammate. Aaron's 120 games played were the fewest since his rookie season. His batting average dipped 62 points to .265, the lowest mark of his career to date. His 34 home runs, while fourth best in the league, were considerably less than the previous year, and his 77 RBIs were also the lowest since his rookie season.

Despite his rocky year, Aaron still passed a series of milestones along the way in 1972. On June 10, Aaron passed Willie Mays for the second spot on the all-time home-run list, connecting for his 649th off Wayne Twitchell in Philadelphia. The bases loaded blast was also Aaron's 14th career grand slam, tying him with Gil Hodges and Wille McCovey for the National League record. Aaron moved into second place on the all-time RBIs list, passing Lou Gehrig by driving in his 1,991st RBI with a solo home run off Mike Corkins in San Diego on June 29. Four days later, he picked up his 2,000th RBI with yet another home run off Houston's Jim York at home in Atlanta. He also equaled Babe Ruth's record for most home runs by a player for one team with his 659th in a Braves uniform on July 19 off Nelson Briles in Pittsbugh. And on July 25, Atlanta hosted the All Star Game and Aaron homered off Gaylord Perry, igniting a home town celebration that Aaron regarded as the biggest ovation he had ever received from the Atlanta fans. On August 4 against the Reds in Cincinnati, Aaron moved past Stan Musial into fourth place with 1,950 runs scored. With a pair of home runs against the Phillies in Atlanta on September 2, Aaron surpassed also Musial's major league record with 6,134 career total bases. And finally, Aaron's home run on September 17 gave him a record of 18 seasons with 100 or more extra bases on long hits.

With 673 home runs at the end of the 1972 season, Aaron's chase for the home-run record was on in earnest. Over the next two years, it would become the singular focus of Aaron and of the baseball world. The Babe's record had stood for thirty-seven years. As Aaron's impending assault on the record became increasingly evident, the baseball community weighed in with its reactions. Inevitable comparisons between Ruth and Aaron were drawn on an almost daily basis and the Bambino's defenders took aim at Aaron. He was barraged with criticism from fans and reporters obsessed with protecting the reputation of baseball's most lovable legend.

In an article titled "Aaron May Set HR Record, Can't Equal Ruth's Slugging" which appeared in the *Boston Globe* on May 14, 1972, reporter Harold Kase conducted an interview with a local statistician and baseball fan named Harold Paretchan. Delivering the kind of criticism that would be levied at Aaron for years to follow, the fan goes on to recite the relative numbers of at-bats it had taken for Ruth and Aaron to reach their home run figures. "Starting this season, Aaron had 10,447 times at bat to Ruth's 8,399. That's about four seasons more," said Paretchan. "Ruth hit a home run in every 11.76 times at bat. Aaron has hit one every 16.35 times up—not even in the all-time first 10."[21]

Aaron also had his supporters. Bob Broeg of the *St. Louis Post-Dispatch* drew his analogies in May 1972:

If Aaron hits more career homers than Ruth's famous 714, it'll be partly because of their lifestyles, which are as contrasting as their color and builds. The white man had a bulging belly long before he quit at 40. The black man is almost as trim at 38 as he when he broke in with the Braves 18 years ago at Milwaukee.

As detailed in the Babe Ruth chapter in Super Stars of Baseball, the Babe would arrive by train from Chicago, say and hightail it over to his favorite St. Louis bordello on Forrest Park boulevard for an evening of booze, babes and black cigars.

By contrast, arriving by plane from Chicago May 4, Aaron checked in at the Chase-Park Plaza hotel, then taxied downtown for dinner at Trader Vic's. "I love Polynesian food," he said.

Afterward he returned to the hotel, watched a television movie and then stayed in bed until past noon the next day. He ordered coffee and newspapers from room service and said, smiling that he spent a couple of hours with TV soap operas.[22]

Aaron sought to squelch the comparisons with Ruth and their resulting controversies. "I've never really read much about him," said Aaron. "From what I do know, the Babe emerges as a big, kindhearted man."[23]

At about this time, Aaron began receiving hate mail at a rate of at least one nasty letter per day from people opposed to the idea of him approaching Ruth's home-run record. One such letter, written in 1972, made its way around the country more than thirty years later as part of the "Baseball as America" touring exhibition put together by the National Baseball Hall of Fame. The actual piece of hand scribbled scrawl is one of thousands like it Aaron received with alarming frequency from anonymous senders.

HANK AARON

Are you trying to show off for your new girl friend.
You must think people or [are] dumb, we know you are trying to break Ruth's record. You dirty old nigger man.
We hope you don't this year. 1973 you will be too dam [sic] old to ever do it. We our club wish you luck all bad luck.
If you think we should honor you Hell now [no] you old slob.
OVER
P.S. Playing ball is better than picking cotton and eating grits—sour Belly

This disturbing sentiment is mild compared to letters that would include threats to kill Aaron and members of his family, the particulars of which were spelled out in specific details, such as the date, time, and location in which they would take place. Many of the letters contained ultimatums calling for him to cease his pursuit of the home-run record.

Perhaps the only other player to share this experience with Aaron was New York Yankees outfielder Roger Maris as he approached and passed Ruth's single-season home-run record of 60 in 1961. "I'd hate to see a bum like Maris break Babe's great record," a letter writer opined to the *Sporting News*. When Maris responded by saying, "I admire Ruth and all he stands for. He was the greatest and there will never be another hitter like him regardless of how many anyone ever hits," it stirred even more ire. "Who the hell does Maris think he is comparing himself to the Babe. What an insult to baseball he is," another resentful fan wrote to the *New York Post*.[24]

Eleven years later Aaron practically echoed Maris' refrain. "I'm not trying to make anyone forget the Babe, but only to remember Aaron," he said. Even Babe Ruth's widow Claire was brought into the fray. "I will not be cheering for him but if he succeeds I will be the first to congratulate him," said Mrs. Ruth. "I don't care how many home runs Aaron or anyone else hits. They cannot replace the Babe. There is no comparison," she said.[25]

Later she also voiced her opinion that Aaron enjoyed the benefit of air travel to Ruth's rails. Aaron responded to Mrs. Ruth's comments with a description of his big league travels. "Remember," he said, "I traveled by train my first few years in the majors, too. By comparisons, those coast-to-coast plane trips and early morning arrivals are a rat race."[26] These early exchanges were just the tip of the iceberg Aaron would be up against and mild compared to the heat he would take as he got closer to the record.

NOTES

1. Jack Mann, "Danger with a Double A," *Sports Illustrated*, August 1, 1966. Emphasis in original.

2. Ibid.

3. Associated Press, "Hank Aaron Excites Fans from Atlanta to Vietnam," April 4, 1967.

4. Aaron, with Wheeler, *I Had a Hammer*, 175.

5. All Dusty Baker quotations are from an interview conducted by the author on June 11, 2003.

6. Author's interview with Don Baylor, May 22, 2003.

7. Ibid.

8. Associated Press, "Hank Aaron Excites Fans from Atlanta to Vietnam."

9. Author's interview with Brooks Robinson, April 3, 2004.

10. Tom Seaver and Marty Appel, *Tom Seaver's All-Time Baseball Greats* (New York: Wanderer Books, 1984), 25.

11. Robert Markus, "Aaron Now Walks in Brilliant Sun, but . . . ," *Chicago Tribune*, September 9, 1969.

12. Ibid.

13. Jim Murray, "Move Over Babe . . . Aaron's Playing Right," *Los Angeles Times*, October, 1969.

14. Wayne Minshaw, "Hank's 3000-Hit Dream Born in '54," *Sporting News*, May 23, 1970.

15. Todd E. Fandell, "Unsung Slugger Baseball's Greatest, Aaron, Speaks Softly But Carries Big Stick," *Wall Street Journal*, April 5, 1971.

16. Minshaw, "Hank's 3000-Hit Dream Born in '54."

17. Samuel A. Andrews, "Bad Henry," *Black Sports*, May/June, 1972.

18. Fandell, "Unsung Slugger Baseball's Greatest, Aaron, Speaks Softly But Carries Big Stick."

19. Aaron, with Wheeler, *I Had a Hammer*, 217.

20. Andrews, "Bad Henry."

21. Harold Kase, "Aaron May Set HR Record, Can't Equal Ruth's Slugging," *Boston Globe*, May 14, 1972.

22. Bob Broeg, "A Comparison of Ruth and Aaron," *St. Louis Post Dispatch*, May 27, 1972.

23. Ibid.

24. Maury Allen, *Roger Maris: A Man for All Seasons* (New York: Donald I. Fine, 1986), 146.

25. Associated Press, November 3, 1972.

26. Broeg, "A Comparison of Ruth and Aaron."

Aaron watches the flight of the ball after his first swing of the new season ties Babe Ruth's record of 714 career home runs in Cincinnati on April 4, 1974. *National Baseball Hall of Fame Library, Cooperstown, N.Y.*

THE CHASE, 1973–1974

On October 14, 1972 in Cincinnati, Jackie Robinson was honored in an on-field ceremony prior to the first game of the World Series between the Oakland A's and Cincinnati Reds. Suffering from diabetes, Robinson was losing his sight and walked with a cane; he appeared much older than his 53 years.

"I'm extremely proud and pleased to be here this afternoon," said Robinson "but must admit, I'm going to be tremendously more pleased and more proud when I look at that third base coaching line and see a black face managing in baseball."[1] It was a sight Robinson would never see. He died ten days later.

Robinson's death put Aaron's own career in perspective. He had come full circle from being a green rookie who idolized Robinson as youngster and looked to him as a role model to becoming not only major league baseball's premier player and elder statesmen, but the primary representative and voice of its black players.

"As I said goodbye to Jackie, I felt more and more like it was up to me to keep his dreams alive," said Aaron. "I figured the chase was the ultimate test of my will. As I moved closer to the Babe I'd remind myself of what Jackie Robinson went through even to the very end he was still trying to kick down those doors."[2]

Tragedy struck again on New Year's Day when it was reported that Pittsburgh Pirates outfielder Roberto Clemente had died in a plane crash attempting to carry supplies to survivors of a major earthquake in Nicaragua. While Aaron hoped for news of Clemente's survival, he was bothered by the petty bickering that had occurred between the two of them over who was the better right fielder;

these exchanges seemed so inconsequential now. Clemente's body was never recovered.

Amidst the turbulence, Aaron found calm with a new romantic interest. Billye Williams was an Atlanta television personality who co-hosted a morning talk show called "Today in Georgia." Aaron and Williams had met a few years before when Aaron was a guest on her show. By 1972, Billye was widowed and Aaron was divorced. Although she declined his first offer of a dinner date, the two became increasingly familiar as Aaron assisted Williams in lining up ballplayers as guests for her show. Billye's previous husband was Dr. Sam Williams, a college professor, minister, and leading civil rights activist who was an adviser to Dr. Martin Luther King Jr. Aaron credited Billye with expanding his mind and consciousness and inspiring him to use his position to improve the lot of blacks in American society. It was shortly after he became involved with Williams that Aaron organized a bowling tournament of major league baseball players and other professional athletes to raise funds for Sickle Cell Anemia research, an event that began a lifelong commitment to improving the condition of black society in America.

Aaron's position had never been more prominent than at the beginning of the 1973 baseball season when the eyes of the world—not just the baseball world—were upon him. And it wasn't just Aaron who was on display; a mirror was also turned on American society. Its response to Aaron's pursuit of Babe Ruth's record reflected a great deal about how far the country had come and still had to go regarding race relations.

Aaron hit his first home run of the 1973 season off Rich Troedson in San Diego on April 11; it was also his first hit of the season after going hitless in his first 11 at-bats. The next day, he knocked another homer off Clay Kirby for number 675; again, it was his only hit of the game. Five days later, he connected off Al Downing in Los Angeles for his third home run and third hit, giving him a .120 average (3-25) after the first nine games of the season. While Aaron was clearly going after the record at this point, he did not want it to come at the cost of his overall production as a hitter. Carrying a .311 lifetime batting average at the start of the season, he was coming off a career-low .268 average in 1972 and wanted very much to get back over .300. This odd slump, during which 7 of Aaron's first 9 hits and 10 of his first 20 went for home runs, continued until May 13 at which time Aaron was batting a paltry .217.

If not for the home runs, this period could have been the most unproductive of his career. Ironically, after nineteen unparalleled and relatively unheralded seasons, the baseball community was recognizing Aaron like never before. Opposing home teams were averaging 10,000 more fans per game when Aaron and the Braves were in town. Oddly enough, the Braves were averaging less than

8,000 fans per game in Atlanta where the home fans were among Aaron's harshest critics. The Braves had gotten off to yet another poor start and during an early May series in Atlanta when crowds were so sparse Aaron recalled "you could practically hear somebody crack open a peanut," a persistent group of hecklers rode Aaron for three straight nights. When derogatory remarks about his batting average and salary culminated in a tirade of racially motivated verbal abuse, Aaron finally reacted. In the ninth inning of the third game, Aaron confronted his tormentors, threatening them with physical violence if their conduct continued. An altercation was avoided when ballpark security intervened and removed the fans from the park, but the incident left an indelible mark on Aaron's memory and caused him to publicly address the poor treatment he was receiving from the home fans. "I've been harassed by a number of fans," said Aaron in post-game comments to the press. "It seems like I'm the whole source that the Braves are in last place. The whole thing's on my shoulders and I don't think it's fair. They're being downright nasty that's all. After 20 years I don't think I deserve it."[3]

The mail continued to pile up to the tune of 3,000 letters per week. For the past few seasons, Aaron had been drawing so much attention that he hired one of the Braves office employees, Carla Koplin, as his own private secretary. Koplin was 22 years old when she began working for the Braves; a year earlier, she had graduated from New York's Katherine Gibbs Secretarial School, which was regarded at the time as the most prestigious in the country.

"In 1970, when his contract came up for renewal he put in a clause that he needed a personal secretary," recalled Koplin years later. A primary duty of Koplin's was dealing with Aaron's multitude of mail. "I opened almost all of the letters," recalled Koplin. "Because of the threatening nature of some, I had to be fingerprinted by the FBI. Any letter that was threatening his life we turned over to the FBI. Of course it was frightening but I also couldn't understand where people were coming from."[4]

Aaron claimed that most of the mail was supportive but enough of it was still filled with poisonous racial invective, specific threats, and hypothetical accounts of how and when they would be carried out to merit serious concern. Although Aaron kept them concealed for some time, many of these letters have since been reprinted in newspapers, magazine articles, and his biographies.

Dear Hank Aaron,

Retire or die! The Atlanta Braves will be moving around the country and I'll move with them. You'll be in Montreal June 5-7. Will you die there? You'll be in Shea Stadium July 6-8, and in Philly July 9th to 11th.

Then again you'll be in Montreal and St. Louis in August. You will die on one of those games. I'll shoot you in one of them. Will I sneak a rifle into the upper deck or a .45 in the bleachers? I don't know yet. But you know you will die unless you retire![5]

The Braves and the city of Atlanta arranged for a local police officer named Calvin Wardlaw to escort Aaron to and from the ballpark, basically serving as a personal bodyguard.

One particularly horrific experience occurred when Aaron was informed by the FBI of a plot to kidnap his oldest daughter, Gaile, who was attending college at Fisk University in Nashville. Another threat on his own life involved a self-described man in a red jacket who wrote that he was going to shoot Aaron during a game in Atlanta. The Braves front office suggested to Aaron that he stay back in the tunnel between the dugout and the clubhouse while the Braves were at bat. Aaron insisted in taking his place on the dugout bench but advised his closest teammates, Dusty Baker and Ralph Garr, that it might be in their best interests not to sit too close to him. "Ralph and I were looking for that red jacket all day," said Baker. "He told us not to sit next to him and we said 'No Hank we're down with you, if you go down, we're going down.' We were scared to death. That motivated him actually. People don't know when you get a strong African American man, threats and idle gossip and propaganda really make him stronger."[6]

This type of behavior and the ceaseless letter writing revealed a depth of emotions and uneasiness regarding race relations in the country that had been lying dormant since the Civil Rights movement reached its height in the late 1960s. Some of it was related to baseball and nostalgia, some of it was racially motivated, and some of it was both. Most of it was vile, born of ignorance and evil.

Dear Nigger,

Everybody loved Babe Ruth. You will be the most hated man in this country if you break his career home run record.

Dear Nigger Scum,

Niggers, Jews, Yankees, Hippies, Nigger Lovers are the scum of the Earth. Niggers are animals, not humans. Niggers do not have souls because they are animals, have strong backs and weak minds. The time has come to send the niggers back to Africa, there is an animal shortage over there. You niggers are no good, sorry dirty as cockroaches and a dead nigger is a good nigger. The nigger loving Jews are sorry as niggers, and a disgrace to the White Race. These scum should be sent back to Israel.

Boy, I despise, hate and detest you scum. The world is better off to get rid of you scum—scum—scum—scum—scum.[7]

Although he had remained quiet about the hate mail during the first few years he had received it, during an early May series in Philadelphia Aaron finally mentioned it to a reporter. His comments drew a note at the bottom of a game story and were soon picked up by the news wire services. A few days later, Aaron's comments were printed in New York and Atlanta, prompting sympathetic responses from fans around the country. Many fans were shocked and dismayed to hear of what Aaron had been enduring. Almost overnight, Aaron began receiving a tremendous outpouring of support from surprisingly unlikely sources, most notably New York, which had previously generated the greatest amount of animosity.

One night at Houston's Astrodome, the Astros posted a message of encouragement to Aaron on its scoreboard.

Mr. Aaron. For every one of those bad letters your receive, there are thousands pulling for you. Good luck in your homer quest . . . after you leave the Astrodome.[8]

Back in Atlanta, Carla Koplin was collecting letters from children.

Dear Mrs. Kopin [sic]

I wish Henry Aaron breaks Ruth's record, and Im sorry of the nasty letters he's getting. I would like Mr. Aaron's autograph and also a strand of one of his Hairs. Enclosed is one of mine. One dirty piece of black hair. Id also want one of yours. I understand if you can't, Because if everybody wanted a strand of his hair, he wouldn't be compared to Babe Ruth, but Yul Brynner.

Thank you[9]

"There was one letter that came and I remember mentioning it to a reporter in one of the stories they did on me," said Koplin.

It was written by a grade school student from a class of underprivileged children in Los Angeles. The students were assigned to write a paper with "I am somebody" as the theme. They had read about what he was going through and applied it to their own situation. I saved one and I can still remember what it said: 'I may be black but I am somebody. I live in a world of mixed colors. I try to understand others and pray they understand me. I will strive to always be somebody

who cares and contributes something to my world.' I pulled that letter because it was heart wrenching.[10]

By the end of the season, Aaron would receive an estimated 930,000 letters
and be presented with a plaque from the U.S. Postal Service for having garnered
more mail, excluding politicians, than any other citizen in the country.

Despite all the attention, or perhaps because of it, Aaron, already a private
person, was forced to keep even more to himself. Years later, when he had a
chance to reflect on this period, he often spoke of feeling like a prisoner in his
apartment or an outcast in his own country. "There are things that happened
to me all through those three years that I've erased from my mind," said Aaron
in an interview for documentary filmmaker Ken Burns.[11]

The stress Aaron was under at the time had both long- and short-term affects
on him. On May 15, 1973, the *Los Angeles Times* ran a story written by Richard Lister, a former professional baseball player turned clinical psychologist, who
warned of the mental anguish and strain the chase could have on Aaron. "It is
my opinion that the psychological demands on Aaron will be more severe than
the physical ones," wrote Lister.

> Some pressures already are evident in Aaron's batting statistics.
> Though he is tied for the major league lead in home runs, his over-
> all average has been around .200. If this wasn't problem enough, the
> team is not winning. . . . A lot of blame is going to fall on the star,
> Aaron. He will be accused of concentrating on personal records at
> the expense of the team . . . Aaron is already manifesting early signs.
> Just a few days ago he tried to go into the stands to shut up an abu-
> sive fan. This type of behavior is surprisingly abnormal for Aaron.
> During his long career he built a reputation for quiet control.[12]

Based on his experience both as a ballplayer and a psychologist, Lister hy-
pothesized that much of the verbal baiting from the fans was probably similar
to what fans had been hollering at Aaron throughout his career. Only now, because of the heightened pressure on him, Aaron was actually listening to what
they were saying. Aaron's reaction to the fans might have been spurred on by
what Lister referred to as paranoia induced by feelings of persecution. Lister predicted things would get worse before they would get better.

> For Aaron, pressures in the form of attention by the fans, press and
> opponents will become more pronounced. The demands will become
> more intense. Sleepless nights may occur more often. Personal relax-
> ation may become but a memory. Food my not taste the same as the

appetite wanes. Hearing may become so acute it may border on ESP, and once-ignored phrases may be taken personally. Media interviews may be irritating by their repetitive queries. And finally, opposing pitchers, may be more cautious and precise with their deliveries, testing Aaron's patience to lay off bad pitches.[13]

By July 11, it was obvious to Lister and to sportswriters around the country that the stress was nearly unbearable. As many as 300 reporters were following Aaron and the Braves on a daily basis.

"I've reached the stage where I wish it was over and done with," Aaron told reporter George Solomon of the *Washington Post*. "I used to love to come to the ballpark. But now I hate it. Every day becomes a little tougher because of all of this. Writers, tape recorders, microphones, cameras, questions and more questions. Roger Maris lost his hair the season he hit 61. I still have my hair," Aaron said. "But when it's all over, I'm going home to Mobile and fish for a long, long time."[14]

In a probing personal interview, Milton Richman, sports editor of United Press International, closed by asking Aaron about life in general. "It's all right I guess," Aaron answered. "If I could just relax a little bit. If I could just get away one day and go fishing. You know how it is being in this position: you're happy to be in it, but you're constantly reminded. The telephone rings, rings, and rings. If you cut it off, it could be the kids (Aaron's four children). You never know. So you leave it on, and all the time it's ring, ring, ring."[15]

About the only place from which Aaron wasn't receiving attention was the commissioner's office. On July 21, Aaron hit number home run 700 off Philadelphia's Ken Brett in Atlanta. After the game, the lucky fan retrieving the ball, 18-year-old Robert Winborne, returned it to Aaron in exchange for 700 silver dollars offered by the Braves. Balls being used in Aaron's at-bats were marked with an invisible infrared ink dot to ensure their authenticity. Winborne's 15 minutes of fame were captured for eternity in a postgame photo session with Hank. While Aaron shook hands with Winborne and smiled for the cameras, he was waiting for a telegram or phone call from the commissioner that never came. Aaron was riled by the fact that Commissioner Bowie Kuhn could not rattle off a wire in that same fifteen minutes. He also sensed a pattern developing that dated back to May 1970 when the commissioner was conspicuously absent in Cincinnati for Aaron's 3,000th hit. Aaron mentioned the slight to reporters, citing what he called his duty to address prejudice and discrimination in baseball. He told the reporters that he believed Kuhn would have shown greater interest in a 700th home run if it had been hit by a white player.

Kuhn said he was waiting to congratulate Aaron at the All Star Game the following week and added that he would be sure to be there whenever Aaron hit numbers 714 and 715. Aaron was still skeptical and Kuhn made a special trip to St. Louis to discuss the situation, explaining that he did not send telegrams to individual players for personal accomplishments because someone might get overlooked. "I didn't think he had to worry about missing somebody who hit 700 home runs, though, since the only other person to do it had been dead for 25 years," said Aaron.[16]

Number 700 was the 27th home run of the year and put Aaron ahead of any pace he had ever set for himself at the season's midway point. Aaron believed 714 was attainable by the end of the season: "I think maybe I can do it this year. I feel that 14 more this season isn't impossible."[17] However, he did not hit another home run for ten days and did not hit number 702 until August 16. Hampered by back spasms, Aaron's pace was decidedly slower in the season's second half; throughout the year, Aaron sat out of games by his own volition, appearing in a career-low 120. "I can't play every day anymore," he told *Sport* magazine. "It's not that you get tired, but your body just doesn't come back as fast as it did. You think you can swing the bat, but you're just a fraction off. The balls you used to hit out of the ballpark you're fouling off. I need more sleep now. Sometimes I'll lie down at 9 P.M. and sleep till 9 A.M."[18]

Despite his feelings of fatigue and the constant scrutiny and pressure, Aaron still managed to put together one of the most productive seasons of his career. Prior to the 1973 season, Aaron averaged 1 home run for every 16 at-bats of his career. During 1973, he hit one every 9 at-bats, a remarkable 40 for the season, the eighth time he had reached that plateau. He hit home runs in three straight games and five out of seven from August 16 to August 28, giving him 706 with a month left in the season. On September 3, he knocked two in a game at home against San Diego.

Five days later, turning to the right page in his book-like brain, Aaron hit 709 by reaching Cincinnati's Jack Billingham for the fourth time in his career. Aaron cataloged the at-bat for future reference. Number 710 came on September 10 off San Francisco's Don Carrithers. With 15 games left to play, Aaron needed four home runs to tie Ruth and five to break his record. It took a whole week and six more games to reach 711, with Aaron connecting off San Diego's Garry Ross in front of a record-low crowd of 1,362 in Atlanta. Only five home games were left on the schedule. The indifference with which Braves fans regarded Aaron during the stretch run of the 1973 season could be attributed to the general apathy with which the city had come to treat the team. But Aaron still felt personally slighted by the hometown fans while the rest of the country was literally singing his praises. New songs were being written about him and receiving radio play; documentary films and prime time network television specials were covering him; *Time* and *Newsweek* featured him on their covers, and a plethora of endorsement opportunities, the likes of which had evaded him throughout his 20-year career, finally came his way. But in Atlanta, the Braves were barely attracting 10,000 fans per game. Aaron attempted to offer reasons for the lack of attention he received in Atlanta.

> The people who cared most about the record were black people, and for the most part they were not the ones who had money to spend at the ballpark. The fans who could afford to come wouldn't, and I believe they missed a lot that year. The only thing ordinary about our team was our record. Phil Neikro pitched a no-hitter in August, and Evans, Johnson and I hit more runs at an unprecedented pace.[19]

Darrell Evans broke in with the Braves in 1969 but had a breakout season in 1973 with 41 home runs. Obtained in an off-season deal with Baltimore, second baseman Davey Johnson knocked a career-high 43 long balls in 1973, finishing just one behind NL leader Willie Stargell. The trio became the first three teammates to hit 40 or more home runs in the same season. Aaron had counseled Johnson early on about using a lighter bat than he had in his previous eight major league seasons, when 18 was the most home runs he had hit in a single season. Aaron therefore took personal pride in Johnson's performance. "At one point, an old lady in tennis shoes stopped me at our hotel in Los Angeles and asked if I were the home run king, and I told her, 'no ma'am, Davey Johnson was up in his room sleeping,'" Aaron recalled.[20]

On September 22, Aaron hit number 712 off Dave Roberts in Houston on the Braves final road trip of the season; the blast placed him two behind Ruth with five games left on the schedule. He sat out the last road game of the season before the Braves returned home for a pair of two-game sets with the Los Angeles Dodgers and Houston Astros. On September 25, Aaron went 0 for 4 as Don Sutton threw a complete game four-hitter and the Dodgers beat the Braves 5–1 in front of 10,211 fans in Atlanta. A paltry 5,500 were on hand the next day as Aaron drove in two runs with a single and a sacrifice fly off Al Downing. The scheduled makeup of a game that ended in a tie between the Dodgers and Braves earlier in the season was rained out on the September 27 and, because it had no bearing on the standings for either team, was not rescheduled, costing Aaron a few more at-bats.

The Astros arrived for the first of a two-game set on the September 29. Approximately 17,000 saw Aaron connect off Jerry Ruess in the first inning for number 713; he went 3 for 4 with three RBIs and moved closer to reaching a .300 average in a 7–0 Braves win.

Aaron's 40th home run completed the Braves trio of 40-home run sluggers and after the game he sat with Johnson and Evans for a special press conference to recognize their historical feat. When every single question was directed towards Aaron and none towards his teammates, he called an abrupt halt to the session and walked away.

The next day, 40,517 showed up and Dave Roberts was on the mound for the Astros in the final game of the season. Having been tagged by Aaron for number 712 the week before, Roberts was very conscious of the dubious opportunity to land his name alongside Aaron's for eternity should he give up another long ball. Aaron did not expect to see many good pitches to hit that day, but, surprisingly, Roberts' first offering came right into Aaron's wheelhouse. Perhaps a little over anxious, Aaron swung too soon, pulling it into foul territory. Given a reprieve, Roberts adjusted his approach to Aaron, throwing him nothing but off-speed pitches on the corners of the strike zone the rest of the day. Aaron did not knock a ball over the wall but did manage three singles, which brought his average over .300 for the first time in the 1973 season. Don Wilson came on in relief of Roberts in the eighth inning and Aaron popped up to second in his final at-bat of the season. When he returned to his position in left field for the top half of the ninth inning, he was greeted by a standing ovation from the fans in the left-field corner of the park. The applause quickly spread around the circumference of Fulton County Stadium. It was the largest crowd of the season and it remained standing and cheering for a full five minutes. The magnitude of the moment caught Aaron off guard. "I couldn't believe that I was Hank Aaron and this was Atlanta, Georgia," remembered Aaron.[21]

In the last postgame press conference of the season, a reporter prefaced a question to Aaron by stating that "Babe Ruth had saved baseball" and wanted to know what Aaron thought he had done for the game. Aaron was not the only one to be taken aback by the question. Author George Plimpton, who was working on a book on the record tying and breaking homers, was also in the room. "It was such a surprising question that a murmur of dismay drifted around the room," wrote Plimpton. Aaron replied, "That's a new one." According to Plimpton's account, Aaron then said, "with just a touch of scorn, 'I haven't done a thing for it.' He turned away for an instant, but then he came back to the question as if it were improper not to make an attempt at it. 'Maybe what I've done is make new fans,' he said quietly. 'At first there was a lot of mail from people, older people, who didn't want me to break Babe Ruth's record. The young generation took note of that, and supported me. I think they want to relate to me, to see me have a record, not someone their granddad saw play."[22]

Aaron finished the 1973 season with 96 RBIs and a .301 batting average, which was especially gratifying considering that he was hitting below .300 for almost the entire season. He would not have to deal with criticism concerning his home runs coming at the expense of batting average, a subject of particular sensitivity to Aaron.

Aaron would have to sit on 713 and wait out the longest, most anxious off-season of his career. Taking his mind off baseball, for a brief while at least, was his marriage to Billye Williams, which took place in Jamaica in November. Shortly thereafter, he adopted Billye's daughter Ceci. "I remember staring at him at the altar and thinking there are not even words to describe how wonderful he was," recalled Ceci.[23]

As wonderful as it all was for Aaron and his new family, the business of baseball was fast approaching and even on his honeymoon he could not help thinking of the task at hand. As recalled in his *I Had a Hammer* memoir, while he was lying on the beach in Jamaica next to his new bride, Aaron thought of Reds pitcher Jack Billingham. The Braves would open at Cincinnati against the Reds and Aaron assumed the Reds would have their ace on the mound. Billingham had won 19 games in 1973 with a 3.04 ERA; he also led the NL with 40 starts (16 of which he completed), 293 innings pitched, and 7 shutouts. Aaron had no trouble remembering that he had tagged Billingham for number 709 on September 8, and he ran the sequence of pitches from each of that day's at-bats on the film projector in his mind. So even though it was his honeymoon, Aaron was thinking about facing Billingham.

But the imminent nature of Aaron's anticipated at-bat against Billingham came into question even before spring training and the exhibition-game season was underway. Braves owner Bill Bartholomay first spoke with Aaron and then publicly suggested that Hank sit out the opening series in Cincinnati so that the historic blasts could be hit in front of the home fans in Atlanta.

The sporting press pounced on Bartholomay's remarks, voicing its opinion that with an Aaron-less line-up the Braves would not be fielding their best nine against the Reds on Opening Day, thereby undermining the integrity of the game. Dick Young of the *New York Daily News* called on Commissioner Kuhn to "come out with a blistering order to the Braves that Hank Aaron must play the first three games, under threat of forfeit." Almost on cue, Kuhn stepped in line and promptly issued an edict to Bartholomay stating that Aaron, based on his previous season's record of service, play in at least two of the three games in Cincinnati or the Braves would be subject to a serious but unspecified penalty.

In a letter dated March 18, 1974, Kuhn, who before becoming commissioner had worked as an attorney for a New York law firm whose clients included the National League, wrote to Bartholomay as follows:

Notwithstanding our disagreement on this subject, I have confidence that you will carry out the requirements of this letter. The only way to do so is to lean over backward in the event of a question arising about his use. Any doubt should be resolved in favor of starting him and continuing to use him in any game. Obviously it would appear very much amiss if he did not start the opening game.

I would have to view any failure to comply with the requirements of this letter as not in the best interests of Baseball, necessitating the imposition of penalties.[24]

A public debate raged in the media during the end of the winter and early spring. "What an outcry this produced," renowned multimedia sports journalist Howard Cosell reminisced in his memoir, *Like It Is*. Echoing sentiments previously expressed by Aaron and Jackie Robinson, Cosell wrote:

The "integrity" of baseball was being challenged. Reams of copy appeared. "Put your best team on the field . . . you must try to win every game. That means Aaron must play." This was the chant. Bowie Kuhn, unparalleled as a man of expedient principle, responded. He ordered that Aaron play in Cincinnati. The "integrity" of the grand old game was thus maintained. Nonsense! *Webster's Unabridged Dictionary* defines integrity as "moral soundness; freedom from corruption. . . ." Where is the moral soundness and freedom from corruption in the carpet bagging, and in the studious avoidance of black managers? And why, instead of only a very occasional article, aren't there reams of copy on these two issues?[25]

Aaron might not have cared all that much about the issue either way if not for the tremendous ovation he received after the final game of the 1973 season. This ovation left a lasting impression on him. He wanted to reward the fans with an attempt at making history for them in Atlanta. He also thought it would be nice to leave a legacy for his family in his new hometown. By the time spring training actually arrived, the press had converged on Aaron and the Braves, creating a three-ring circus atmosphere in anticipation of home runs 714 and 715, regardless of where they would be hit. Braves manager Eddie Mathews could not avoid being brought into both the Opening Day flap and the media swarm around Aaron. "I don't like to use the word nightmare," recalled Mathews, "but they just overwhelmed everybody, but Hank just went on being Hank."[26] Throughout the duration of the spring season, Aaron was kept in a separate undisclosed location, living in a private penthouse apartment.

As Opening Day approached, Aaron realized he would indeed be in the starting line-up and his thoughts returned to Billingham. And Billigham's thoughts returned to Aaron. On the eve of the opener, a tornado whipped through Cincinnati and its surrounding areas. As if the prospect of surrendering 714 to Aaron the next day was not enough to cause insomnia, Jack Billingham tried to catch forty winks on the floor of his basement at home in the nearby suburb of Delhi, while storm winds blew shingles off the roof.

According to an interview with author George Plimpton, Billingham said there was almost no talk of Aaron or the upcoming game around the breakfast table with the exception of a lone utterance of concern from Billingham's father to which Billingham responded: "Dad just cool it. I'm going out there to do my best. If I have a bad day, please don't get upset about it."[27]

On the morning of April 4, 1974, Aaron awoke to the news that more than 30 people could have died as a result of the evening's storm. Bowie Kuhn flew in for the game on Air Force Two with Vice President Gerald Ford. Along the way, Ford instructed the pilot to fly over the city of Xenia, Ohio, which had been hit particularly hard by the tornado. Ford was standing in for President Richard Nixon, who was fully embroiled in the Watergate scandal.

Aaron arrived at the ballpark early for an extended pregame press conference during which he took the opportunity to introduce a Hank Aaron Scholarship Fund sponsored by Western Union. The company would donate one dollar for every telegram Aaron received after tying and breaking the record. He also used the podium to ask the Reds to honor the sixth anniversary of the assassination of Dr. Martin Luther King with a moment of silence.

A residual fallout from the prior evening's weather was a stiff wind whipping around the circumference of Cincinnati's Riverfront Stadium, a possible omen of bad tidings for Billingham, a sinkerball pitcher whose livelihood relied on keeping the ball low and getting ground ball outs. If Aaron could get his bat under one of Billingham's deliveries, a strong wind could provide enough added lift to carry the ball over the fence.

Cincinnati Reds rookie broadcaster Marty Brennaman, who was making his big league debut behind the microphone, has vivid recollections of the day, including its weather conditions. "I worked a full spring training schedule but that was my first regular season game in 1974 and the day before we had devastating tornadoes in Ohio that destroyed property and took some lives," said Brennaman. Up in the booth, the broadcaster was feeling the excitement of the moment. "Everybody knew," recalled Brennaman, "that Henry was sitting on 713."[28]

Billingham took the mound and promptly succumbed to the obvious pressure, or perhaps simply adapted to his place in the drama. Considered a control pitcher, Billingham averaged less than 60 walks per season in his 13-year career, but he walked free-swinging Ralph Garr (who averaged less than 20 free passes per season during his 13-year career) on four straight pitches to lead off the first inning. Maybe it was nervousness or just the cold, damp weather. The next batter, Mike Lum, singled and Garr stood at second. Darrell Evans flied out to left field and the crowd erupted as Aaron moved from the on-deck circle towards home plate.

The crowd was already restless after the first offering and a low murmur hummed from the seats when he missed again for ball two. The next pitch was a fastball for a called strike, not what Aaron was looking for. "I went up there looking for a sinker, and I wasn't going to swing until I saw it," said Aaron.[29] When Billigham missed again for another ball, the crowd booed in unison. "I just won 19 games the previous year and I go to three and one on Hank and people start booing me," said Billigham, "everyone wants to see it," he said to himself.[30]

According to Billingham, the next pitch was a fastball, which in his case usually behaved like a sinker. It moved in on Aaron. "Not a bad pitch," said Billingham later, "but it was too good a pitch for Henry Aaron."[31] It happened abruptly on Aaron's first swing of the season. Amidst all the anticipation, anxiety, and controversy, Aaron hit a low line drive that carried just far enough to make it over the wall in the left-field corner. It didn't even reach the fans in their seats, landing in a moat-like no man's land, where a specially deployed policeman retrieved it and was promptly instructed to place it in a brown paper bag held by a grounds crew attendant.

Aaron made his way quickly around the bases, a little faster than his usual flat-footed trot. At home plate, he was greeted first by a mob of his teammates and then by Reds catcher Johnny Bench, who squeezed in a slight congratulatory gesture. After breathing the first big sigh of relief for the season, Aaron was handed a microphone to the public address system and made a very brief statement: "Thank you very much, I'm just glad it's almost over with." Vice President Gerald Ford and Commissioner Bowie Kuhn also delivered short speeches before play resumed. Ford was appreciative of what Aaron and his home-run quest had done for the morale of American citizens. "Millions of Americans had lost faith in their government and the White House because of the tragedy of Watergate and the tragedy of the war in Viet Nam," Ford later recalled.[32] Off to the side of the ceremony an uncomfortable Billingham tried to stay loose, throwing warm up tosses to Bench. In frustration, he threw with increasing velocity and after a while started yelling audibly, "Let's get going, let's Go!"[33]

There was still the matter of the rest of the game to play. Aaron grounded out in the third, walked and scored in the fifth, and flied out to center in the seventh. Afterwards, Rowland Office replaced him in the batting order. The Reds went on to win the game 7–6 in 11 innings. After the game, Aaron fielded questions from the press and took a moment to acknowledge the anniversary of the death of Dr. King while also mentioning the request he had made of the Reds organization for a public recognition. "Actually today was the day that Dr. King was killed. We were a little disappointed," said Aaron with his wife Billye standing at his side, "I requested we have a moment of silence and for some reason they found that their schedule didn't permit them to, today, and I was just a little disappointed."[34]

Billye also spoke up during the press conference, coming to Aaron's defense when she believed the reporters' questioning of Aaron regarding his request concerning Dr. King had taken an antagonistic tone. "Before I knew it, I was talking. I blurted out something to the effect that he shouldn't have even had to ask for the moment of silence and that we should take the occasion to remember Dr. King," said Billye Aaron.[35]

The controversy surrounding Aaron's playing time in Cincinnati continued the next day when Mathews kept him out of the line-up and said he had planned on keeping him out of the next game as well. Again the commissioner came down hard. "To say I was annoyed at the Braves would grossly understate the situation," said Kuhn.[36] Mathews recanted his previous statement. "The commissioner has unlimited powers to impose very serious penalties on individuals or the ballclub itself. For the first time I realize that these penalties are not only fines but also suspensions and other threats to the franchise itself. Because of this order and the threatened penalties, I intend to start Hank Aaron tomorrow," said Mathews.[37] Aaron played, but went 0 for 3 with two strikeouts against Cincinnati hurler Clay Kirby. He was incredulous later when reporters suggested he might have been tanking it.

The next day in Atlanta, another chapter was added to the ongoing saga between Aaron and the commissioner. Kuhn opted not to show up for the Braves home opener, citing a prior commitment to address the Wahoo booster club in Cleveland and a desire not to have his presence be a distraction at the ballpark. Aaron felt his absence was even more disturbing than his presence would have been and again felt slighted by the commissioner. In his stead, Kuhn sent former Negro League star and New York Giants Hall-of-Fame center fielder Monte Irvin, who worked in the commissioner's office. The Braves honored Aaron with a pregame ceremony modeled after the "This is Your Life" television program.

Aaron's first manager, Ed Scott from the Mobile Bay Black Bears, stood above Alabama on a map of the United States that had been drawn on the field. John Mullen, who signed Aaron to his first contract, was there as well, as was Charlie Grimm, his first manager in the majors, and career-long pal Donald Davidson. Celebrities such as Pearl Bailey, who sang the National Anthem, Sammy Davis Jr., and Redd Foxx occupied front row seats, as did Georgia governor

Jimmy Carter. The only conspicuous absentees were President Richard Nixon, whom Aaron would forgive, and the commissioner, whom he could not. Wearing, like Aaron, number 44, was the Los Angeles Dodgers starting pitcher Al Downing, a 13-year veteran with 115 wins under his belt.

In the pregame ceremony, Aaron told the sell-out crowd of more than 53,000 that he hoped to get it over with that night; in the clubhouse before the game Aaron told his teammates that he would. He didn't have much of a chance in his first at-bat. With the entire crowd standing and cheering, Downing was obviously rattled by the magnitude of the occasion; he was wild outside of the strike zone, walking Aaron on five pitches, none of which registered a twitch from Aaron's bat. The restless and anticipatory crowd booed. Dusty Baker followed with a double to score Aaron. On a night when everybody came to see him move into first place on the all-time home run list, it almost went unnoticed that it was the 2,063rd run of his career, moving him past Willie Mays with the most runs scored in National League history.

With the Braves down 3–1, Aaron came to the plate again in the fourth after Darrell Evans reached first on an error to lead off the inning. Again the crowd rose to its feet and the frenzied cheering increased with each pitch. It was possibly the loudest crowd in Atlanta baseball history. Downing's first pitch bounced in the dirt and the crowd booed lustily. "And that just adds to the pressure," said Dodgers broadcaster Vin Scully, who was also being heard by a national audience. "Downing has to ignore the sound effects and stay a professional and pitch his game."[38]

Satch Davidson, the home plate umpire, discarded the ball and the first base umpire, Frank Pulli, threw another specially marked ball to Downing as if the pitcher needed further reminder of drama of his situation. Downing's next offering was a low slider straight down the middle of the plate. For the first time in the game, Aaron got his bat in motion and met the ball just in front of the plate. Like 714, it took off on a low line causing Dodgers shortstop Bill Russell's knees to buckle for an instant as he stopped just short of leaping up for the ball. It kept on rising and left fielder Bill Buckner gave chase all the way to the fence, which he grabbed to vainly pull himself up. The ball eluded his reach and was caught in the Braves bullpen by relief pitcher Tom House. Aaron watched it all the way, not sure if he had hit the ball hard enough. But it seemed everyone else in the ballpark knew he did as the crowd erupted, competing with the sound of fireworks blasting off from behind the home run wall.

As Aaron circled the bases, he was joined by a pair of college kids who somehow managed to evade ballpark security. Aaron's bodyguard, Calvin Wardlaw, had to size up the situation and immediately evaluate its potential danger, his hand postured above the snub nose .45 he held in a binocular case. The young men ran along each side of Aaron as he made his way around second and towards third base patting him on the back before he gently nudged them away. Rounding third and heading for home with a smile spreading across his face, Aaron was met at home plate by the entire Braves team. Ralph Garr took hold of Aaron's leg and made sure Hank's foot touched home plate. Tom House had been sprinting from the bullpen and almost beat Aaron home, sticking the historic ball hard in the palm of Hank's hand.

"What a marvelous moment for baseball, what a marvelous moment for Atlanta and the state of Georgia, what a marvelous moment for the country and the world," broadcast Scully to the nation. "A black man is getting a standing ovation in the Deep South for breaking the record of an all-time baseball idol. And it is a great moment for all of us and particularly for Henry Aaron who was met at home plate not only by every member of the Braves but by his father and mother. He threw his arms around his father and as he left the home plate area his mother came running across the grass, threw her arms around his neck, kissed him for all she was worth."[39]

Although her son was surrounded by his teammates, Aaron's mother Estella made a beeline through the mob and locked a bear hug around his neck. Aaron remembered her squeezing him so hard that he couldn't believe her strength. Afterwards, she revealed her reasons for holding on so tight and not letting go. She remembered the threats which said that if Aaron did break the record he would never make it to home plate alive. Recalling the moment later, she said if her son were going to be shot by a sniper they would have to shoot her first. "With any luck I could die with him. Let me go down with him, me and him go together," said Estella Aaron.[40]

The game was halted for yet another on-field ceremony. Aaron was again handed a microphone and said simply and succinctly, "Thank God it's all over with."[41] A light rain shower sprinkled the field during the ceremony. Had it persisted enough to halt play after just four innings, it would have meant it was not an official game and number 715 might have been erased from the historical record. But the rain diminished and the game continued. Downing walked the next two batters and was removed from the game. The Braves scored two more runs to take a 5–3 lead. Aaron came up again in the fifth and seventh innings, grounding out both times. In the top of the eighth, Aaron was taken out of the game and replaced in the line-up by Rowland Office. After the game, Mathews closed the clubhouse to everyone except the players and their family members. Champagne was poured and Mathews stood on a table and proposed a toast to the best ballplayer he had ever seen.

During its next day's session, the United States Congress recognized Aaron's accomplishment with testimonials delivered by no less than twelve members of

the House of Representatives and Senate. The Senate unanimously passed reso-
lution 305 stating: "Therefore, be it resolved that the United States Senate
hereby extends its congratulations to Henry Aaron in recognition of this singular accomplishment."[42]

Aaron dominated a docket that included a suggestion that actress Jane Fonda
renounce her American citizenship after her controversial visit to North Vietnam as well as a report on racial progress in South Africa. In addition to their
accolades, many of the members of Congress also submitted newspaper articles
to be printed in the *Congressional Record*. The Honorable Andrew Young of
Georgia delivered the following address:

> Mr. Speaker, the late Dr. Martin Luther King, Jr., once observed that
> in a world filled with people seeking attention and acclaim, once in
> a while we will find a humble man "who forgets himself into im-
> mortality."
>
> Such a man is Henry Aaron, who last night achieved immortality
> by breaking the greatest record in all of sport. . . .
>
> Through his long career, Hank Aaron has been a model of hu-
> mility, dignity, and quiet competence. He did not seek the adoration
> that is accorded to other national athletic heroes, yet he has now
> earned it. He did not allow the abuse against him and his fellow black
> athletes to deter him from his historic purpose.[43]

Young also submitted two articles from the *Atlanta Constitution* written by
Jesse Outlar. Under the headline " 'Hammer' Flips a Page in History," Outlar
began: "It was a cool, rainy April night in Atlanta, the kind of weather in which
Bowie Kuhn probably would not have ordered Henry Aaron to play, but more
than 50,000 in the stadium and millions in TV-land won't ever forget that he
did."[44]

In the second story submitted by Young, writer Charlie Roberts quoted Georgia Governor Jimmy Carter as asking: "Where was Commissioner Bowie Kuhn,
and did the New York press tell him not to come? Hank's a great gentleman
and completed a great era here tonight. I feel like Atlanta, the Braves and Hank
have been insulted by his absence."[45]

A Washington Post editorial printed on April 6 was also inserted into the
Record:

> But Aaron has given something else to the national life: an emotional
> relief from the number of tragedies and absurdities that now domi-
> nate the news and much of our consciousness. Here is a person who
> is authentic, whose acclaim is based on the results of his self-

confidence and not self-promotion, who has been faithful to his vocation whether noticed or not. At a time when so many national events cast common citizens into doubts and confusions about what has really happened beneath the surface of the news, a profound reassurance is provided by Hank Aaron.[46]

Aaron took the day off on April 9 and then broke his own record with number 716 on April 11 off yet another Dodgers pitcher, Charlie Hough. Two months later, Congress' Flag Day Committee, which honors prominent Americans whose talents have made significant contributions to the American way of life, made its first such presentation to an athlete in a ceremony honoring Aaron on June 13, 1974.

"So it is a great honor for me to come here before the Congress on this special occasion," said Aaron, "as I have always had great respect for the Flag and what it symbolizes. To me the Flag has been more than just merely an inspiration. In my more than 20 years of professional baseball I have seen the Flag waving in every ball park from legendary Ebbets Field and the Polo Grounds to the new sports complexes around the National League. Ever since my first game in Eau Claire in the Northern League in 1952, I have been aiming at the Flag in more ways than one."[47]

With the pressure of the chase behind him, Aaron settled into what could be seen as a victory lap around the league. Playing less than one-third of the Braves schedule, he would come to the plate 340 times in 112 games. Speculation about everything from whether he would retire or be traded at the end of the season to the possibility of being offered a front office or field manager job fed the rumor mill throughout the waning months of the season.

In what would be his last at-bat in an Atlanta uniform, Aaron hit his 20th home run of the season in the seventh inning of the Braves last game of the year, establishing a record of 20 straight 20-home run seasons that brought his total to 733. Overwhelmed by the uncertainty of his situation and overcome by emotion, he did not emerge from the dugout to tip his cap. Aaron was disappointed that there were only 11,000 people in the park to see the last of his 3,076 games with the Braves, which at the time was the record for one player with the same team. Just like Ruth, who ended his career in a Boston Braves uniform wondering if he would be offered a manager's job, it was time for Hank and the Braves to part ways. Despite his topsy-turvy relationship with the city, Aaron had left a lasting legacy in Atlanta.

Thirty years later, President Jimmy Carter, who was governor of Georgia during much of Aaron's time with the Braves, offered his assessment of Aaron's place in Atlanta's history: "With his moral integrity, forbearance in the face of racial abuse, and his mastery of the game of baseball, Hank Aaron was a heroic and effective pioneer in the Civil Rights movement in Atlanta and throughout the South."[48]

By the time he had finished playing in Atlanta, what Henry Aaron left behind concerned so much more than baseball. "Look, I don't have the vision or the voice of Martin Luther King or James Baldwin or Jesse Jackson or even of Jackie Robinson. I'm just an old ballplayer, said Aaron. "But I learned a lot as a ballplayer. Among other things, I learned that if you manage to make a name for yourself—and if you're black, believe me, it has to be a big name—then people will start listening to what you have to say. That was why it was so important for me to break the home run record. Believe me, there were times during the chase when I was so angry and tired and sick of it all that I wished I could get on a plane and not get off until I was some place where they never heard of Babe Ruth. I had to break that record. I had to do it for Jackie and my people and myself and for everybody who ever called me a nigger."[49]

In his book *The Black 100*, a ranking of the most influential African Americans, Columbus Salley claims Aaron was selling himself short when he said he lacked "the vision or voice" of other civil rights advocates. Salley acknowledges that Aaron had indeed made a conscientious decision to use the home-run record to "further advance the causes of freedom and equality for African-Americans much as Muhammad Ali used the heavyweight title."[50] Together, the two dominated the American sports scene from April through October 1974 in ways that reached far beyond their athletic arenas. Six months after Aaron passed Ruth, Ali knocked out George Foreman in Kinshasa, Zaire, on the African continent capturing the heavyweight championship title for the second time. "The only man I idolize more than myself is Henry Aaron," said Ali.[51]

NOTES

1. Tollin, *Hank Aaron, Chasing the Dream*.
2. Tollin, *Hank Aaron, Chasing the Dream*.
3. *Henry Aaron: The Life of a Legend* (Revere, MA: Fleetwood Recording Co., Inc., 1974).
4. Author's telephone interview with Carla Koplin in 2003.
5. Aaron, with Wheeler, *I Had a Hammer*, 237.
6. Author's interview with Dusty Baker on June 11, 2003.
7. Aaron, with Wheeler, *I Had a Hammer*, 230, 234.
8. Musick, *Hank Aaron*, 180.
9. Baldwin and Jenkins, *Bad Henry*, 77.

10. Author's telephone interview with Carla Koplin in 2003.

11. Ken Burns, *Baseball* (Washington, DC: WETA-TV, Florentine Films, 1994).

12. Richard Lister, "Psychologist Claims Aaron's Bid for Record Affecting Hank," *Los Angeles Times*, May 15, 1973.

13. Ibid.

14. George Solomon, *Washington Post*, referenced in the *Atlanta Constitution*, July 11, 1973.

15. Milton Richman, "The Trials of Henry Aaron: 'Everyday, It's the Same,' " *Atlanta Constitution*, July 11, 1973.

16. Aaron, with Wheeler, *I Had a Hammer*, 247.

17. Musick, *Hank Aaron*, 193.

18. *Sport* magazine, September 24, 1973, 73.

19. Aaron, with Wheeler, *I Had a Hammer*, 251.

20. Ibid., 232.

21. Ibid., 254.

22. George Plimpton, *Hank Aaron: One for the Record* (New York: Bantam Books, 1974), 20.

23. Tollin, *Hank Aaron, Chasing the Dream*.

24. Bowie Kuhn, *Hardball: The Education of a Baseball Commissioner* (New York: McGraw-Hill, 1988), 120.

25. Howard Cossell, *Like It Is* (Chicago: Playboy Press, 1974), 135.

26. Tollin, *Hank Aaron, Chasing the Dream*.

27. Plimpton, *Hank Aaron*, 12.

28. Author's interview with Marty Brennaman, May 22, 2003.

29. Aaron, with Wheeler, *I Had a Hammer*, 262.

30. Tollin, *Hank Aaron, Chasing the Dream*.

31. Plimpton, *Hank Aaron*, 29.

32. Tollin, *Hank Aaron, Chasing the Dream*.

33. Plimpton, *Hank Aaron*, 30.

34. Tollin, *Hank Aaron, Chasing the Dream*.

35. Aaron, with Wheeler, *I Had a Hammer*, 264.

36. Kuhn, *Hardball*, 123.

37. Ibid.

38. Vin Scully from NBC radio broadcast, April 8, 1974.

39. Ibid.

40. Tollin, *Hank Aaron, Chasing the Dream*.

41. Ibid.

42. Congressional Record—House, April 9, 1974.

43. Ibid.

44. Ibid.

45. Ibid.

46. Ibid.

47. Ibid., June 13, 1974.

48. President Jimmy Carter, letter to the author, March 9, 2004.

49. Aaron, with Wheeler, *I Had a Hammer*, 4.

50. Columbus Salley, *The Black 100: A Ranking of the Most Influential African-Americans Past and Present* (Secaucus, NJ: Carol Publishing Group, 1999), 317.

51. *Ultimate Sports Presents Kings of Swing: Baseball's Greatest Home Run Hitters* (Davenport, IA: Ultimate Sports Publishing).

BACK TO MILWAUKEE AND BEYOND

Six weeks after Henry Aaron hit his historic blasts, 7,000 miles to the east, Sadaharu Oh of the Yomiuri Giants in the Japanese major leagues knocked his 600th career home run. At season's end, the pair met for a home run hitting contest in Japan. By this time, 40-year-old Aaron had hit 733 home runs to 34-year-old Oh's 634. At their current paces, it was evident that Oh would probably hit more career home runs than Aaron.

"There the comparisons stopped for me," said Oh. "He played in America and I did not. I knew enough of American baseball to know what his record meant," reflected Oh in his memoir, *A Zen Way of Baseball*, coauthored with David Falkner. Aaron won the contest hitting 10 home runs to Oh's 9. "It was an honor to be on the field with this great champion, but I did not compare myself with him," said Oh who would eventually surpass Aaron by 113 with a career total of 868. "His numbers, yes, his accomplishments no. Winning the contest was important for many fans in Japan, and I tried my best to accede to their wishes. I might have won, but I didn't. The importance of my being there was in the fact that some people recognized that I played the game in a certain way, at a certain professional level. All along that had been my secret source of pride."[1]

Like Aaron, Oh, whose name translated means "king," was no stranger to adversity in the forms of prejudice and discrimination. Of mixed ethnic origin, Oh, whose father was Chinese, was subject to taunts and verbal bashing that were similar to what Aaron had received throughout his career. During an extended slump lasting almost three seasons, Oh recalled hearing a chant from

A bronze statue of Aaron outside Fulton County Stadium in Atlanta. The statue was later moved to the new Turner Field where it remains. *National Baseball Hall of Fame Library, Cooperstown, N.Y.*

more than one crowd across the league, "Oh! Oh! Sanshin Oh!" [King! King! Strikeout King!]. Said Oh, "A friend or two over the years has maintained that I heard it only because I was not a full-blooded Japanese."[2]

While in Japan, Aaron received a telephone call from Bud Selig, an old friend from Milwaukee, a car salesman during Aaron's days with the Milwaukee Braves and current owner of the American League's Milwaukee Brewers. At 3:00 A.M. Japanese time, Selig woke Aaron in his hotel room to inform him that he had been traded to the Brewers for outfielder Dave May and a minor league pitcher named Roger Alexander.

Aaron was ecstatic at the prospect of returning to the site of his greatest glories. Unlike the ups and down he experienced in Atlanta, Aaron's relationship with Milwaukee was one of mutual admiration and affection. A few weeks later, he signed the most lucrative contract of his career, a two-year deal worth nearly half-a million dollars. Selig also sweetened the deal with talk about the possibility of an executive position with the club and a Schlitz beer distributorship when Aaron's playing days were through.

It was obviously his last deal as a player. The designated-hitter rule adopted by the American League in 1973 was still in its experimental phase, but Aaron was almost the prototype for the position: an aging slugger, not so light on his feet as he used to be but with some pop remaining in his bat.

Accentuating the feeling of homecoming that Aaron felt upon his return was the fact that Del Crandall, a former teammate of Aaron's with the Milwaukee Braves, was the Brewers manager. Aaron served almost as a coach for his new teammates, many of whom were a generation younger than he was. For the team's emerging slugger, first baseman George Scott, Aaron served as a mentor. "I had the best season of my career that year, and I believe it was because of Hank Aaron—not only the fact that he batted in front of me, but because of the way we used to sit and talk about baseball," said Scott.[3]

As early as spring training, manager Crandall had Aaron conducting hitting clinics for the team. On Opening Day, the largest crowd in the Brewers' five-year history—48,000—showed up to greet its new old hero. Aaron collected a base hit and an RBI and a few days later connected off his old nemesis, Gaylord Perry, for his first American League home run. But the luster of his new uniform began to wear off quickly and by the end of the season's first month, Aaron was looking every bit of his 41 years. Struggling to keep his average above .200, his knowledge of the game and his situational hitting still enabled him to drive in runs and to rapidly encroach on yet another of Ruth's records. Amidst little fanfare, Aaron, with a two-run double on April 27, tied the Babe with RBI number 2,211. On May 1, in a 4-for-4 outing, Aaron singled off Detroit's Vern Ruhle, scoring Brewers teammate Sixto Lezcano with the RBI record breaker.

No extra out-of-town writers were present to cover the game and neither was Commissioner Bowie Kuhn. With few mile markers ahead of him, Aaron struggled to find a motivational driving force and, like Ruth, Rogers Hornsby, and Willie Mays—aging heroes who returned to the cities that made them stars—Aaron found there was no new formula for success. But like the other aging stars before him, fans still wanted to see Aaron play. On the road, the Brewers were a big draw. Despite a batting average hovering below .250 and a power shortage that would end in a 12–home run season, Aaron was still voted to the All-Star team for the twenty-first straight season. He was more than just a ballplayer now. He was a media celebrity and television personality. Reunited with yet another former Milwaukee teammate, he joined Brewers broadcaster and resident funnyman Bob Uecker for his daily pregame show.

"Hank was always a friend," Uecker reminisced when he was inducted into the broadcaster's wing of the Hall of Fame in Cooperstown in 2003. "We used to do the pregame show together for Magnavox and laugh. That's all we did was laugh; he wouldn't do the show unless I did it with him. I was broadcasting in Milwaukee in his last years and we did that show every day."[4]

At a time when Uecker was enjoying being the center of attention and entertaining the media, fans, family, and friends during his induction weekend, he took a serious pause to reflect on Aaron:

> Hank Aaron came up in a totally different time, in times that were totally tougher I think. There were eight teams in each league, there were no playoffs and all this stuff. And to do what Henry did and for the length of time. Today's guys if they do it will be in a shorter period of time. But for Henry to persist and go through the things he did racially, when he approached the record. People who weren't around Hank don't know how bad that was, how tough that was. Hank Aaron is somebody all by himself. I don't care what happens today with Bonds, McGwire or anybody else.[5]

Uecker has been an outspoken supporter of Henry Aaron, who he feels has not been properly recognized for his achievements. "I never say anything about Babe Ruth," Uecker told Me and Hank author, Sandy Tolan. "If I say anything it's about Henry Aaron. Babe Ruth doesn't have a [the home run] record anymore," said Uecker.[6] "I don't want to sound like I'm knocking Babe Ruth. Babe Ruth was a legend. But when I talk about records and home runs—Henry Aaron is the guy. That's it!"[7]

Aaron's last blast, the record number 755, came midway through the following season off Dick Drago of the California Angels in Milwaukee on July 20. At 42, nagged by chronic injuries to his back and knee as well as deteriorating vision, Aaron would have only a few more at-bats during the rest of the 1976 season. Number 755 was his 10th of the year; he would drive in 35 runs in 85 games with a career low .229 average. He crossed the plate 22 times, the last of which landed him in a dead even tie with the Babe at 2,174 for second on the all-time list behind Ty Cobb. Rickey Henderson eventually passed all three in 2001.

Before the 1976 season was finished, Aaron had already announced that he would accept a position as director of player development with the Atlanta Braves for new owner, Ted Turner, the television mogul. By this time, Selig's Schlitz deal had gone sour, with Aaron being offered territory in Baltimore instead of as expected in Atlanta.

On the last day of the 1976 season, Aaron beat out an infield single in the last of his 12,364 at bats, driving in his 2,297th run; both were record numbers at the time, although Pete Rose has since come to bat almost 2,000 more times. At the time of this writing, Aaron still holds the records for career home runs, RBIs, total bases, and extra base hits, and is second in at-bats and third in games played (3,298) and hits (3,771).

Aaron speculated almost prophetically on the possibility of someone breaking his home-run record immediately after he set the mark. "Records are made to be broken," Aaron said to reporters in the Braves clubhouse. "I'm hoping that in my time, before I die, I see some kid come along, black or white, come along and challenge or break my record."[8]

Almost 30 years later, San Francisco Giants outfielder Barry Bonds went from 500 to 600 home runs faster than any other player, earning serious consideration as heir to the home-run king's throne. Aaron himself gave Bonds a vote of confidence and even appeared in a television commercial as a voice over a public address system at a ballpark urging Bonds to consider his retirement plans. In the August 12, 2002 issue of *USA Today*, Aaron was quoted as saying, "I wish Barry well. I told him to go for everything that he can, because it doesn't last forever."[9]

At about the same time, accusations of steroid use in baseball had become common headlines in the sports pages of the country's newspapers and sports magazines. The story reached epic proportions during the pre-season of 2004. Much of the speculation was aimed at Bonds, who was linked to a San Francisco Bay area fitness center accused of supplying professional athletes with steroids.

In an interview conducted by Don Walker of the *Milwaukee Journal Sentinel* and published on March 5, 2004, Aaron expressed concern about the far-reaching effects of steroid use on professional athletes. "Whether you want to be or not, you are a role model," Aaron said. "When you are playing sports these kids idolize you. They will do just like you."[10]

Early in the 2004 season, when Bonds hit his 660th home run to pass Willie Mays, Aaron was asked for his opinion on whether Bonds' career home run total would be tainted if it was proved he used steroids.

> I'll let the public judge for themselves; I'm just hoping and praying nothing comes up. I admire Barry Bonds. Steroids or no steroids, he would have had a Hall of Fame career. At one time I thought Ken Griffey Jr. had the best chance to break my record, but injuries have hounded him. Barry Bonds has done everything—hit home runs, steal bases, hit for average. He's practically carried his ball club on his back.[11]

In the three decades that followed his departure from the game as a player, Aaron has worked in the Atlanta Braves front office and has continued to champion the cause of African Americans in their pursuit of careers in baseball both on and off the field. Although there were times that Aaron felt slighted or passed over from being given serious consideration for a field manager's position, he was twice offered the job of Braves manager by Ted Turner—once, right after his first year of working as director of player development in 1977, and again a few years later. Both times Aaron declined the offer. Noting that Frank Robinson had already broken the barrier, Aaron said if he felt at the time that it would have been important for a black man to have the position he would have taken it.

In 1982, five years after his retirement as a player Aaron was elected with Frank Robinson to the Baseball Hall of Fame. They shared the dais on their day with former commissioner Happy Chandler, who in 1947 had voted against 15 of 16 major league owners to force the integration of baseball. During his induction speech, Chandler recounted the events leading up to his decision. He remembered the words he spoke in a private conversation with Branch Rickey: "I'm going to have to meet my maker someday and if he asks me why I didn't let this boy play, and I said because he was black. That might not be a satisfactory answer."[12]

Frank Robinson recalled breaking into the big leagues two years after Aaron and being well aware of the reputation Aaron had already began carving for himself.

> I think he made me a better baseball player . . . because when Hank would get up with the Milwaukee Braves—hit a home run, I'd be standing in the outfield watching it go over. I said, well this is up to you when you get up there you got to try to do something as well if not as good because your teammates are going to be expecting the

same. My neck got sore watching Hank Aaron's fly balls go over the fence . . . it's been said that he didn't get his just dues as a player and I agree, because Hank Aaron was not a flashy individual. He just went about his job and did it very well.[13]

For his part, Aaron kept his speech short but sweet, first acknowledging those who came before him. "I feel especially proud to be standing here where some years ago Jackie Robinson and Roy Campanella proved the way and made it possible for Frank and me and for other blacks in baseball."[14]

A short while later he summed up his career succinctly: "I stand here today because God gave me a healthy body, a sound mind and talent. For 23 years I took the talent that God gave me and developed it to the best of my ability. Twenty-three years ago I never dreamed this high honor would come to me. For it was not fame I sought, but rather to be the best baseball player I could possibly be."[15]

Aaron continued in his capacity as the Braves player development director, coordinating scouting reports, signing players, and organizing teams. Although the Braves suffered through some lean years during his tenure, such notable players as Dale Murphy, Tom Glavine, and Dave Justice rose up through the system under his watch.

Since 1989, Aaron has served as senior vice president and assistant to the president while sitting on the board of directors for both the Braves and the WTBS television station. He has also been a board member for the NAACP, the Leukemia Society of America, the Sickle Cell Foundation of Georgia, and the Mutual Federal Savings and Loan.

Aaron has been a baseball executive for so long now he is regarded as being among the game's foremost dignitaries, diplomats, and ambassadors, as well as an unofficial spokesperson on racial issues. In 1999, major league baseball created the Hank Aaron Award to honor the best overall hitter in each league. But like the way Aaron and his career existed off the mass media radar, the award has received little recognition, even though it is intended to be the hitter's equivalent to the Cy Young Award. Writing for The *New York Times*, John Rosenthal attempted to draw some distinction to the award a few weeks after its 2003 presentation. "But five seasons after that award's inception it carries none of the prestige of the MVP award. Even the most knowledgeable baseball fans don't commit the winner's names to memory. . . . Newspapers barely report it. The *Times* has not carried an article devoted to it since 2000," wrote Rosenthal.[16]

When the Braves hosted the 2000 All Star Game in Atlanta, Aaron took the opportunity to address an issue of sensitivity regarding the Braves name, logo, and tomahawk chop chant. Aaron said to members of the news media that if these things were offensive and hurtful to Native Americans than they should be changed, including the name of the team he worked for.

Periodically, Aaron has been mentioned as a possible commissioner of baseball, a position he would have used to push for minority hiring in front office positions. Aaron publicly proclaimed his candidacy when Bowie Kuhn resigned in 1984. Eventually, Peter Ueberoth, a millionaire California travel agent and organizer of the 1984 Summer Olympics in Los Angeles, was named to the post. "They certainly weren't looking for a baseball man or champion of minorities— which I found out firsthand when I met with Bud Selig and two other search committee members to interview for the position before Ueberoth was hired," said Aaron.[17]

Aaron never felt that he was given serious consideration for the position and while acknowledging that he would have needed some help understanding some of the business aspects of the job, he thought he had a huge leg up on the baseball end of it. "It struck me as ironic that baseball was saying blacks didn't have the experience for front office jobs, and yet they hired consecutive commissioners who had no background in baseball," said Aaron. "Although I had some serious reservations about Ueberoth, I thought Giamatti was on his way to becoming an excellent commissioner before his tragic death."[18]

A few years later, when A. Bartlett Giamatti was promoted from National League president to commissioner there was speculation that Aaron would replace Giamatti. "My name is always mentioned. They always mention my name but nobody ever calls me," said Aaron to a group of reporters in Scottsdale, Arizona, while working on a corporate fundraiser for the Big Brother/Big Sisters of America. "I think baseball is making a superficial attempt to bring in more minorities. I don't think that they're making a genuine attempt," said Aaron.[19]

On more than one occasion Aaron has spoken out on major baseball issues with a more authoritative voice than that of the commissioner. After first coming to the defense of Pete Rose, saying he believed Rose's claims to have never bet on baseball, Aaron changed his stance when Rose later admitted to gambling in a 2004 memoir. "I just think it is hogwash to say that he should be put back into the game just because the public wants it," Aaron said. "A rule is a rule, and the rule is on every clubhouse door that you can't bet on baseball. It doesn't say that you're excluded if you have 4,000 hits or 700 home runs."[20]

During the same off-season (2003–2004), baseball's steroid scandal reached a crescendo with the announcement that several major league players, including Barry Bonds, were being indicted by a federal jury in the investigation of the Bay Area Laboratory Co-operative (BALCO) nutritional substance lab. While commissioner Bud Selig issued an industry wide gag order and most players held their tongues for fear of breaking ranks with their union, Aaron was one of the few to voice an opinion. "I think the union has done a marvelous job for the players," Aaron said. "But the protections that have been given to the players are uncalled for."[21]

After more than a dozen years in the Braves front office, Aaron began pursuing numerous business interests outside baseball. Some ups and down included a real estate misadventure in the mid-1970s that cost him nearly $1 million, the equivalent to his life savings. Fortunately, he still had his name and fame and signed a five-year $1 million endorsement contract with Magnavox towards the end of his playing career. He also worked as a spokesperson for the Arby's fast food restaurant chain when Arby's was an official sponsor of major league baseball. Aaron later parlayed this relationship into his first major post-baseball business venture, acquiring a dozen Arby's franchises in the Milwaukee area. Although he later sold those restaurants, he has remained in the fast food business as owner of more than a dozen-and-a-half Church's and Popeye's fried chicken outlets and a Krispy Kreme doughnut shop. He operates these businesses, which are collectively part of his 755 Restaurant Corporation, from his headquarters at Hank Aaron BMW, one of six auto dealerships he oversees in Atlanta. With $76.7 million in sales, Aaron was named *Black Enterprise* magazine's 2004 Auto Dealer of the Year.

Aaron remains a senior vice president with the Braves but spends much less time at the ballpark than he did in his previous capacity in player development. Aaron's interest is, of course, piqued when spring training rolls around each year but he feels a certain communication, if not generation, gap between himself and modern ballplayers. "Some of the players these days, they walk in with a suitcase full of money and a cell phone against their head—I can't tell them anything," said Aaron to the *Atlanta Journal Constitution* on the eve of his 70th birthday in February 2004.[22]

Over the years, the anniversary of both 714 on April 4, 1974, and 715 four days later have become recognized as holy days of obligation among the baseball faithful and, coming as they do on or around Opening Day every year, lend themselves well to celebration. On April 8, 2004, 30 years to the day after he hit number 715, Aaron was honored by the Atlanta Braves in a pregame ceremony. He was asked to recall his thoughts and feelings at the time of the chase and he reiterated what he had been saying then and ever since. "It should have been the greatest time of my life, but it was the time that I couldn't wait was over. It was something I didn't have fun with," said Aaron. However, with each passing year he seems to have come to terms with the experience and even to have reconciled himself with the feelings of anger he once associated with the record. "I'm beyond that stage. I've always said that the person walking around with resentment and hate is a defeated person. I'm a long ways from being defeated."[23]

After the pregame ceremony, Aaron joined the Braves broadcasters in the booth for a couple of innings. After the requisite small talk, the discussion moved to the state of the game and its most prominent problem—the steroid issue. Seizing the opportunity, Aaron spoke up.

> Yes, it hurts me very much. It has set baseball back, especially with a player such as Bonds who's been the greatest athlete in the last seven years. He can carry a team on his shoulders. I said it before, if anybody breaks it I hope it is Barry. But this is causing problems among young people. I think that MLB, the union and the players, have got to take a hard line. If somebody has tested positive bring it to light. Bring them out. Get them out of the way and let's get on with it. Baseball has been divided for such a long time, the owners, the players, the union. Let's get this thing over with. I love baseball. I still love it. I don't know of anything I'd rather watch. I don't want the fans to give up on us.[24]

For all the misconceptions of a man who was supposed to have gone about his business quietly, at 70 Aaron continued to dispel such notions and showed no signs of being a man ready to go quietly into that good night.

NOTES

1. Sadaharu Oh, with David Falkner, *Sadaharu Oh: A Zen Way of Baseball* (New York: Vintage Books, 1984), 22.

2. Ibid., 86.

3. Aaron, with Wheeler, *I Had a Hammer*, 292.

4. Interview with Bob Uecker in Cooperstown, NY, July 27, 2003.

5. Ibid.

6. Ibid.

7. Tolan, *Me and Hank*, 58.

8. Henry Aaron, *The Life of a Legend*.

9. Mel Antonen, "600 Down, 156 to Go, Bonds Has Serious Shot at Aaron's Home Run Record," *USA Today*, August 12, 2002.

10. Don Walker, "Hammerin' Away, Aaron Takes Swing at Players' Union in Drug Fiasco," *Milwaukee Journal Sentinel*, March 5, 2004.

11. Dave Anderson, "Aaron Content to Let the Fans Judge Bonds' Achievements," *New York Times*, April 7, 2004.

12. Albert B. "Happy" Chandler, from his Hall of Fame induction speech, August 1, 1982, Cooperstown, NY.

13. Frank Robinson, from his Hall of Fame induction speech, August 1, 1982, Cooperstown, NY.

14. Hank Aaron, from his Hall of Fame induction speech, August 1, 1982, Cooperstown, NY.

15. Ibid.

16. John Rosenthal, *New York Times*, October 2003.

17. Aaron, with Wheeler, *I Had a Hammer*, 326.

18. Ibid.

19. Hank Aaron, from an interview in Scottsdale, AZ, August 1992.

20. Associated Press, January 1, 2004.

21. Don Walker, "Hammerin' Away, Aaron Takes Swing at Players' Union in Drug Fiasco."

22. Jim Auchmutey, *Atlanta Journal Constitution*, February 6, 2004.

23. Guy Curtwright, "'Mr. Brave' Honored at Turner Field," *Atlanta Journal Constitution*, April 8, 2004.

24. Hank Aaron, from a television interview on WTBS, April 8, 2004.

Newly crowned home-run king Aaron addressing Congress on Flag Day, June 14, 1974. © *Bettmann / CORBIS*.

EPILOGUE:
"THEY SAY I'M BITTER"

The paradox of Henry Aaron's multifaceted personality and the almost schizophrenic portrayals of him that zig-zag through the historical record of his life are most apparent in his two authorized autobiographies. The first, *Aaron, r.f.*, was written with *Atlanta Journal Constitution* baseball beat reporter Furman Bisher in 1968; the book was revised with a new "Afterword" chapter and retitled *Aaron* in 1974. In this autobiography, Aaron comes across as quiet and unobtrusive, not wanting to rock the boat, perpetuating the image of him that had been presented to the public up to that point.

In the Bisher book, as he begins to recount a racist situation involving an attempt to exclude his father from a dinner in which Aaron was supposed to be the guest of honor, Henry said, "I'm no crusader, not in the way they use the word now. Never wanted to be. Let's get that straight before we go any further."[1]

In a preamble to his account of the horrific situation he endured as one of the first black men to integrate the South Atlantic League, Aaron wrote, "I ought to point out here that just getting to the major leagues didn't eliminate segregation. You know I don't like that word. Every time I use it, it makes me feel like I'm complaining. I feel like I'm charging somebody with a crime. I don't feel that way at all. This country has been good to me and I've had a great life."[2]

In stark contrast, in *I Had a Hammer*, published in 1991, Aaron and his coauthor Lonnie Wheeler set out in the book's introduction to dispel the notion perpetuated throughout Aaron's career that he rarely spoke out on social issues until the period surrounding his pursuit of the home run record. "But Aaron maintained that he had stepped forward on racial issues throughout his career, and the old articles bear him out; he was on record in behalf of black managers and desegregated training camps as far back as the late 1950s."[3]

By the time *I Had a Hammer* was published, Aaron had a lifetime of stereotypical depictions of himself to turn around. Early newspaper and magazine feature articles on Aaron sounded condescending even when they attempted to flatter or praise him. "Aaron, soft spoken when he speaks at all, followed the suggestions that Negro players in their first venture in the Deep South league should pay attention solely to the application of their own talents to the game," wrote Milwaukee newspaper writer Joe Livingston in 1953.[4] If these characterizations of Aaron quietly going about his business were lacking in charisma, they soon gave way to the racially charged creations of Aaron as a "stepanfetchit" shuffler. As he began to put up the numbers that would make him a star in his first few years in Milwaukee, he was typecast as a carefree country bumpkin with feature stories appearing under such headlines as " 'Slow Motion' Aaron Becomes Colorful Figure in Braves Camp."[5]

Picking up on the sleepy, drowsy, lazy themes developed in earlier stories, a 1958 *New York Times Magazine* article referred to Aaron as a "slow-moving, somnolent type," although "never asleep at the plate," and a "somniferous (*adj*. Inducing sleep)-looking young man," who "when he is not swinging a bat . . . is moving about—or, better yet, standing still—with a leisurely air of awesome proportions."[6]

The writer continued to pursue the angle of Aaron playing in some sort of subconscious state by using an embarrassing isolated incident to support his thesis. "As a base runner, his most memorable achievement came when he doubled into a double play. After watching him shuffle, head down and oblivious to all about him, until two runners were out, a coach lectured him: 'Henry, you've got to watch the ball or the coach when you're running the bases and you've got to decide when the ball goes out to the outfield whether you should tag up and go to another base or hold your base.' Henry's answer was simple and definitive: 'I can't do all that.' "[7] The misappropriated use of the word "achievement" regarding Aaron's base-running skills seems especially sarcastic in reference to a player who hit 14 triples in 1956 and another 6 in 1957.

In the next paragraph, the writer offers a possible analysis of Aaron's behavior that, whether or not it was delivered with malicious intent, would continue to plague Aaron throughout his playing days. "Actually, Aaron . . . is possessed of a rich, sly, dry humor: there are those who suspect his apparent indolence is his own private joke on the human race. 'Tell you the truth,' one of his minor league bosses has said, 'we couldn't make up our minds if he was the most naïve player we ever had, or whether he was dumb like a fox.' "[8] And so Aaron's relative quiet was portrayed as really just a part of his clever charade, deadpanning his inner jokester.

"White folks think of us as entertainers, that we're born to entertain them," Aaron said upon the April 1995 release of *Chasing the Dream*, a documentary film of his life. "They expect us to smile, laugh at things that ain't funny. Baseball is part of that. It was all right for me to hit home runs because I entertained them. It wasn't all right for my kids to go to school with their children."[9]

By 1969, as he was approaching the twilight years of his career, a few of the more thoughtful members of the sportswriting fraternity sought to make more probing inquiries towards an accurate portrayal of Aaron's multifaceted persona. Phil Musick of the *Pittsburgh Press*, who would later write *Hank Aaron: The Man Who Beat the Babe* (1974), one of the more lyrical biographies on Aaron, addressed Aaron's personality in a June 9, 1969, column: "Great guy, the baseball people say of Aaron, a credit to his race and the game, as if a man is ever a credit to anything but himself. Colorless they say. Great ballplayer but no pizzazz. Too bad he could have made a million."[10]

Musick agreed with certain aspects of this assessment, citing Aaron's golden rule treatment of others; however, he drew the line on Aaron's quiet side pertaining to matters of race and quoted Aaron in support of this argument. "'I get tired of hearing about a Negro manager's qualifications,' growled Aaron, slightly out of character and a bit angry at the suggestion that the Jackie Robinsons and Roy Campanellas might not have been ready to run a big-league team at the end of brilliant careers."[11]

In the May-June 1972 issue of *Black Sports* magazine, writer Samuel A. Andrews also discussed the dichotomy of Aaron's nature.

> Henry Aaron is a very private personal individual. Somehow, amidst the hundreds of articles written about him and his exploits, Henry has managed to separate himself from the madding crowd. And because of his reticence to seek the public spotlight, his pronouncements, when in evidence, carry that much more weight. His statements are as deep as the outfielders who seek to defend against the line drives rocketing off his bat.[12]

Andrews also quoted Aaron as follows:

> We haven't made any progress at all. The Black ballplayer has got to make the owners know about things. If you don't speak out, you don't get anything. I don't think we've said nearly enough, especially the established ballplayer, myself included. As long as I can do things

because I am a ballplayer, then I've got to speak up. . . . Right now, we're organizing Black athletes to get something together to help fight Sickle Cell Anemia. This organization is part of the Pittsburgh organization with guys like Doc Ellis, Muhammad Ali and Willie Stargell. And sometimes, the white people are more helpful than many Blacks. Governor Jimmy Carter of Georgia and Senator Ted Kennedy have both been very helpful. We've got to push things; let everybody know how we feel.[13]

After many years of toiling in relative obscurity in the small media markets of Milwaukee and Atlanta (before the latter became an international business and media center), the spotlight was turned on Aaron with unrelenting frequency during the two baseball seasons in which he was chasing Ruth's record. Twenty years after his big league debut, the baseball community and the American news media tried to fathom his legend.

A 1974 *Ebony* magazine article written by Alex Poinsett tried to explore Aaron's historical depiction.

Meanwhile, white newsmen, lacking the patience or sensitivity to interview him in depth, have pictured him as a rather simple-minded young man, a quiet colored boy gifted with a singular skill. It was perhaps a comforting image to white baseball fans, but a cruel caricature which Aaron bitterly resented but bore—like his father would have—without a whimper.[14]

But Aaron certainly didn't whimper and he didn't mince words either. As he became more confident and self assured, he developed his voice and used his stature among the elite ballplayers of his generation to speak out when he saw injustice. Early in his career, he called for the baseball establishment to integrate living conditions during spring training. Later, he asked baseball owners to consider blacks as managerial and front office candidates and questioned why black players of equal or greater skill than their white counterparts were not paid accordingly. In the years following his retirement, once again experiencing this type of discrimination first hand, his voice became louder regarding these same issues. This came as a surprise to the image crafters who promptly gave him a personality makeover. The new media incarnation described Aaron as angry, ungrateful, and bitter, a depiction that remains a persistent image of Aaron.

On January 31, 1980, *Atlanta Constitution* writer Lewis Grizzard reassessed his opinion of Aaron, one week after Aaron refused to accept an award for giving baseball its greatest moment because he still felt slighted by Commissioner Bowie Kuhn's handling of the days surrounding his breaking of Ruth's record.

"The writers used to write of Henry Aaron, 'This man quietly goes about his job of being everybody's superstar.' But oh Henry how you have changed," wrote Grizzard. "Before you hit No. 714 to tie the Babe's record in Cincinnati, you sounded off because of the fact that it was the anniversary of Dr. Martin Luther King's death. Suddenly, you're Henry Aaron activist. Who put you up to that Jesse Jackson?"[15]

As far as his image was crafted by others, Hank Aaron couldn't win. Henry Aaron was indeed a shy and quiet teenager. Early portrayals of Aaron in the minor leagues and when he first entered the major leagues paint an oversimplified picture of a personality that was more complex than it appeared on the surface. Had Grizzard checked the record, he would have found out that Aaron had been an activist all along but had not been afforded the public platform that became more readily available after he broke Ruth's record and later as he became organizational executive and baseball industry dignitary.

As Aaron wrote later, "I make it my business not to be content. Of course, that rubs some people the wrong way. They say that I'm bitter. They say that I have a chip on my shoulder, that I read racism into every phrase and discrimination into every decision. But I don't think white people can understand that I have a moral responsibility to do whatever I can."[16]

While confusing to some members of the news media, Aaron's message was not lost on all. In a June 10, 1993, column under a headline reading, "Home Run King Aaron Not Bitter, Just Honest," Art Spander of the *San Francisco Examiner* attempted to explain Aaron's motivation. "Aaron hit more home runs than anyone in major league history, 755. He is an American icon. To some he is an American irritant. They're the ones who want their heroes agreeable not angry, appreciative not demanding. They're the ones who made his journey into history a trip of agony." Spander also cited Aaron's San Francisco speech to the National Association of Minorities in Cable. Aaron told the group that there were not enough of minorities in visible positions of power, but he also urged them to not give up and keep up the fight. "If that sounds like the words of somebody who is a malcontent, well, reminds Aaron, if one person in this land is prevented from fulfilling his potential simply because of ethnic background, then there is a reason for discontent," wrote Spander. " 'I don't think people ever understood me,' said Aaron, by nature a gentle person until challenged. 'I read little tidbits always saying that I'm angry or bitter or a racist. I'm just the opposite. But you have to remember where I came from, what I went through' "[17]

Two years later, William Rhoden of the *New York Times* reiterated Aaron's sentiments in an April 9, 1995, column entitled, "It Is Time We Took Aaron Into Hearts." Write Rhoden: "But for all this, Aaron has never been taken into the American bloodstream in the manner of Babe Ruth the man whose home run record he broke in 1974. By contrast no one really knew or for that matter knows Henry Aaron as anyone except for the solemn, steady pursuer and claimant of Ruth's career home run record."[18]

By the end of the 1990s, Aaron had largely moved away from baseball. Although retaining a position as a senior vice president with the Atlanta Braves, the lion's share of his time and attention were devoted to his numerous business dealings. "I knew I couldn't play baseball for 40 or 50 years, so I always had my eye on the bigger picture," Aaron told *Black Enterprise* magazine in June 2004. "I believed if I could just get into something and keep it growing I could do well. That's when I looked at myself and said I was a businessman."[19]

Despite his departure from baseball as a daily part of his of life, Aaron remains close enough to the industry to be constantly called upon for his opinions and commentary. Aaron speaks out where others are afraid to tread, especially on controversial subjects, such as the lack of executive and managerial positions for minorities in baseball and the issue of steroid use in baseball.

"This game is bigger than Babe Ruth, bigger than me or Ted Williams," Aaron said to the *Milwaukee Journal Sentinel* on March 5, 2004. "This is a game that belongs to everybody in the world. We need to be concerned about the problem of steroids . . . The kids think that if they take steroids, they will be successful in sports. It's not so much that it's one player taking it. But we owe it to the kids to do the right thing."[20]

As Barry Bonds began to approach Aaron's home run record in 2003 and 2004, the sporting press ironically came to Aaron's defense, much like they did for Ruth a generation earlier. On September 4, 2003, MLB Web site columnist Mike Bauman claimed that while Bonds may be able to set a new record, Aaron was a more fitting king.

> Henry Aaron endured much, from the beginning of his career to almost the end. In a very real way, he deserves this record, not only for his talent, but for the burden he had to carry.
>
> Moving into the 21st century, what has Barry Bonds had to endure on a regular basis? The media. The questions. The intrusions. The loss of privacy. Without minimizing any of its trauma, it does not seem to be a mountain of travail compared to what Henry Aaron lived through.
>
> What I am left with here is basically the notion that Henry Aaron was a more important and more put upon historical character than Barry Bonds and thus is more deserving of this most coveted record.[21]

With the same perseverance he exhibited as a player, Aaron, since retirement, has continued to preach his mantra of hard work and its just rewards. He has insisted on using the prestige that comes with his accomplishments as a launching pad to speak out against prejudice, oppression, and discrimination. He carries himself with a stately posture and dignified bearing and, although he keeps a watchful eye over his shoulder, a smile regularly adorns his visage.

NOTES

1. Aaron, with Bisher, *Aaron*, 27.
2. Ibid., 38.
3. Aaron and Wheeler, *I Had a Hammer*, xi.
4. Joe Livingstone, *Milwaukee Journal*, October 25, 1953.
5. Sam Levy, "'Slow Motion' Aaron Becomes Colorful Figure in Braves Camp," *Milwaukee Journal*, March 21, 1954.
6. William Barry Furlong, *New York Times Magazine*, September 21, 1958.
7. Ibid.
8. Ibid.
9. William Rhoden, *New York Times*, April 9, 1995.
10. Phil Musick, *Pittsburgh Press*, June 9, 1969.
11. Ibid.
12. Samuel A. Andrews, *Black Sports*, May/June 1972.
13. Ibid.
14. Alex Poinsett, *Ebony*, July 1973.
15. Lewis Grizzard, *Atlanta Constitution*, January 31, 1980.
16. Aaron and Wheeler, *I Had a Hammer*, 3.
17. Art Spander, *San Francisco Examiner*, June 10, 1993.
18. William Rhoden, *New York Times*, April 9, 1995.
19. Tanisha Sykes, *Black Enterprise*, June 2004.
20. Don Walker, *Milwaukee Journal Sentinel*, March 5, 2004.
21. Mike Bauman, MLB.com, September 4, 2003.

APPENDIX: HENRY AARON'S CAREER AND POST-SEASON STATISTICS

CAREER STATISTICS

Year	Club	League	G	AB	R	H	2B	3B	HR	RBI	BA	PO	A	E	FA
1954	Milwaukee	National	122	468	58	131	27	6	13	69	.280	223	5	7	.970
1955	Milwaukee	National	153	602	105	189	37	9	27	106	.314	340	93	15	.967
1956	Milwaukee	National	153	609	106	200	34	14	26	92	.328	316	17	13	.962
1957	Milwaukee	National	151	615	118	198	27	6	44	132	.322	346	9	6	.983
1958	Milwaukee	National	153	601	109	196	34	4	30	95	.326	305	12	5	.984
1959	Milwaukee	National	154	629	116	223	46	7	39	123	.355	263	22	5	.982
1960	Milwaukee	National	153	590	102	172	20	11	40	126	.292	321	13	6	.982
1961	Milwaukee	National	155	603	115	197	39	10	34	120	.327	379	15	7	.982
1962	Milwaukee	National	156	592	127	191	28	6	45	128	.323	341	11	7	.980
1963	Milwaukee	National	161	631	121	201	29	4	44	130	.319	267	10	6	.979
1964	Milwaukee	National	145	570	103	187	30	2	24	95	.328	284	28	6	.983
1965	Milwaukee	National	150	570	109	181	40	1	32	89	.318	298	9	4	.987
1966	Atlanta	National	158	603	117	168	23	1	44	127	.279	315	12	4	.988
1967	Atlanta	National	155	600	113	184	37	3	39	109	.307	322	12	7	.979
1968	Atlanta	National	160	606	84	174	33	4	29	86	.287	418	20	5	.991
1969	Atlanta	National	147	547	100	164	30	3	44	97	.300	299	13	5	.982
1970	Atlanta	National	150	516	103	154	26	1	38	118	.298	319	10	7	.977
1971	Atlanta	National	139	495	95	162	22	3	47	118	.327	733	40	5	.996
1972	Atlanta	National	129	449	75	119	10	0	34	77	.265	996	70	17	.987
1973	Atlanta	National	120	392	84	118	12	1	40	96	.301	206	5	5	.977
1974	Atlanta	National	112	340	47	91	16	0	20	69	.268	142	3	2	.986
1975	Milwaukee	American	137	465	45	109	16	2	12	60	.234	2	0	0	1.000
1976	Milwaukee	American	85	271	22	62	8	0	10	35	.229	1	0	0	1.000
Major League Totals—23 years			3298	12,364	2174	3771	624	98	755	2297	.305	7436	429	144	.982

156

Post-Season Statistics

Year	Round	Club	G	AB	R	H	2B	3B	HR	RBI	BA
1957	World Series	Milwaukee	7	28	5	11	0	1	3	7	.393
1958	World Series	Milwaukee	7	27	3	9	2	0	0	2	.333
1969	NLCS	Atlanta	3	14	3	5	2	0	3	7	.357
Totals			17	69	11	25	4	1	6	16	.362

A = assists; AB = at-bats; BA = batting average; E = errors; FA = fielding average; G = games; H = hits; HR = home runs; PO = put-outs; R = runs; RBI = runs batted in; 2B = doubles; 3B = triples

Awards and Records

1956 NL Highest Batting Average .328; NL Most Hits 200

1957 NL MVP; NL Most Runs Scored 118; NL Most Home Runs 44; NL Most RBIs 132

1959 NL Highest Batting Average .355

1960 NL Most RBIs 126

1963 NL Most Runs Scored 121; NL Most Home Runs 44; NL Most RBIs 130

1966 NL Most Home Runs 44; NL Most RBIs 127

1967 NL Most Runs Scored 113; NL Most Home Runs 39

1st All-Time in Home Runs 755

1st All-Time in RBIs 2297

1st All-Time in Total Accumulated Bases 6856

2nd All-Time in At-Bats 12,364

3rd All-Time in Hits 3771

3rd All-Time in Runs Scored 2174

3rd All-Time in Games Played 3298

SELECTED BIBLIOGRAPHY

BIOGRAPHIES AND AUTOBIOGRAPHIES OF HANK AARON

Aaron, Hank, with Dick Schaap. *Home Run: My Life in Pictures.* Kingston, NY: Total Sports, 1999.

Aaron, Henry, with Furman Bisher. *Aaron.* 2nd ed. New York: Thomas Crowell, 1974.

Aaron, Henry, with Lonnie Wheeler. *I Had a Hammer.* New York: HarperCollins Publishers, 1991.

Baldwin, Stan, and Jerry Jenkins. *Bad Henry.* Radnor, PA: Chilton Book Company, 1974.

Cohen, Joel. *Hammerin' Hank of the Braves.* New York: Scholastic Book Services, 1973.

Musick, Phil. *Hank Aaron: The Man Who Beat the Babe.* New York: Associated Features, 1974.

Plimpton, George. *Hank Aaron: One for the Record.* New York: Bantam Books, 1974.

Tolan, Sandy. *Me and Hank: A Boy and His Hero, Twenty-Five Years Later.* New York: Free Press, 2000.

BOOKS

Adelson, Bruce. *Brushing Back Jim Crow: The Integration of Minor-League Baseball in the American South.* Charlottesville: University of Virginia Press, 1999.

Allen, Maury. *Roger Maris: A Man for All Seasons.* New York: Donald I. Fine, 1986.

Berra, Yogi. *The Yogi Book: I Really Didn't Say Everything I Said!* New York: Workman Publishing Co., 1998.

Cosell, Howard. *Like It Is.* Chicago: Playboy Press, 1974.

Creamer, Robert W. *Babe: The Legend Comes to Life.* New York: Penguin Books, 1983.

Degregorio, William A. *The Complete Book of U.S. Presidents.* 3rd ed. New York: Barricade Books, 1991.

Ellison, Ralph. *Invisible Man.* New York: Random House, 1952; Quality Paperback Book Club edition, 1994.

Garner, Joe. *And the Crowd Goes Wild: Relive the Most Celebrated Sporting Events Ever Broadcast.* Napierville, IL: Sourcebooks, 1999.

Holway, John. *The Sluggers.* Alexandria, VA: Redefinition Books, 1989.

Hoppel, Joe. *The Series: An Illustrated History of Baseball's Post Season Showcase.* St. Louis: The Sporting News Publishing Co., 1992.

Kuhn, Bowie. *Hardball: The Education of a Baseball Commissioner.* New York: McGraw-Hill, 1988.

Lacy, Sam, with Moses J. Newson. *Fighting for Fairness: The Life Story of Hall of Fame Sporstwriter Sam Lacy.* Centreville, MD: Tidewater Publishers, 1998.

Lester, Julius. *Look Out Whitey! Black Power's Gon' Get Your Mama!* New York: Grove Press, 1968.

Mead, William, and Paul Dickson. *Baseball: The Presidents' Game.* New York: Walker and Company, 1997.

Moffi, Larry, and Jonathan Kronstadt. *Crossing the Line: Black Major Leaguers, 1947–1959.* Iowa City: University of Iowa Press, 1994.

Oh, Sadaharu, with David Falkner. *Sadaharu Oh: A Zen Way of Baseball.* New York: Vintage Books, 1985.

Peterson, Robert. *Only the Ball Was White: A History of Legendary Black Players and All-Black Professional Teams.* New York: Oxford University Press, 1992.

Ribowsky, Mark. *The Power and the Darkness: The Life of Josh Gibson in the Shadows of the Game.* New York: Simon and Schuster, 1996.

Riley, James A. *The Biographical Encyclopedia of the Negro Baseball Leagues.* New York: Carroll and Graf Publishers, 1994.

Salley, Columbus. *The Black 100: A Ranking of the Most Influential African-Americans Past and Present.* Secaucus, NJ: Carol Publishing Group, 1999.

Seaver, Tom, and Marty Appel. *Tom Seaver's All-Time Baseball Greats.* New York: Wanderer Books, 1984.

Seymour, Harold. *The People's Game.* Oxford: Oxford University Press, 1990.

Tackach, James, and Joshua B. Stein. *The Fields of Summer: America's Great Ballparks and the Players Who Triumphed in Them.* New York: Moore and Moore Publishing, 1992.

Ward, Geoffrey C., and Ken Burns. *Baseball: An Illustrated History.* New York: Alfred Knopf, 1994.

Williams, Juan. *Thurgood Marshall: American Revolutionary.* New York: Times Books, Random House, 1998.

STATISTICAL REFERENCES

The Baseball Encyclopedia: The Complete and Definitive Record of Major League Baseball. 10th rev. ed. New York: Macmillan, 1996.

Dickson, Paul. *The Dickson Baseball Dictionary.* New York: Facts on File, 1989.

Johnson, Lloyd, and Brenda Ward. *Who's Who in Baseball History.* New York: Brompton Books Corp., 1994.

Solomon, Burt. *The Baseball Timeline: The Day-by-Day History of Baseball, from Valley Forge to the Present Day.* New York: Avon Books, 1997.

INTERVIEWS AND LETTERS

Baker, Dusty. Interview with author, June 11, 2003.

Baylor, Don. Interview with author, May 22, 2003.

Brennaman, Marty. Interview with author, May 22, 2003.

Carter, Jimmy. Letter to author, March 9, 2004.

Klimchock, Lou. Interview with author, February 2003.

Koplin, Carla. Telephone interview with author, 2003.

Robinson, Brooks. Interview with author, April 3, 2004.

Torre, Joe. Interview with author, September 28, 2003.

Uecker, Bob. Interview in Cooperstown, NY, July 27, 2003.

ARTICLES

Aaron, Hank, with Jerome Holtzman. "Are You Ready for a Negro Manager? I Could Do the Job." *Sport*, October 1965.

Anderson, Dave. "Aaron Content to Let the Fans Judge Bonds' Achievements." *New York Times*, April 7, 2004.

Andrews, Samuel A. "Bad Henry." *Black Sports*, May/June 1972.

Antonen, Mel. "600 Down, 156 to Go, Bonds Has Serious Shot at Aaron's Home Run Record." *USA Today*, August 12, 2002.

Associated Press. "Hank Aaron Excites Fans from Atlanta to Vietnam." *Atlanta Journal Constitution*, April 4, 1967.

Auchmutey, Jim. "It's Good to Be King." *Atlanta Journal Constitution,* February 6, 2004.

Broeg, Bob. "A Comparison of Ruth and Aaron." *St. Louis Post Dispatch*, May 27, 1972.

"Clowns Test Stars at Stadium Sunday." *Baltimore Afro-American*, May 17, 1952.

Curtwright, Guy. " 'Mr. Brave' Honored at Turner Field." *Atlanta Journal Constitution*, April 8, 2004.

Davids, L. R. "Rookie Aaron Sets All-Time Major First Alphabetically." *Sporting News*, April 28, 1954.

Fandell, Todd E. "Unsung Slugger Baseball's Greatest, Aaron, Speaks Softly But Carries Big Stick." *Wall Street Journal*, April 5, 1971.

Furlong, William. "The Panther at the Plate." *New York Times Magazine*, September 21, 1958.

Grizzard, Lewis. "What Made 'Hammer' into 'Bad Henry?'" *Atlanta Constitution,* January 31, 1980.

Krupinski, Joe. "Move to Georgia Peachy? Not to Aaron." *Milwaukee Journal*, October 22, 1964.

Levy, Sam. "'Slow Motion' Aaron Becomes Colorful Figure in Braves Camp." *Milwaukee Journal*, March 21, 1954.

Lister, Richard. "Psychologist Claims Aaron's Bid for Record Affecting Hank." *Los Angeles Times*, May 15, 1973.

Livingston, Joe. "Braves Teen Age Hopefuls." *Milwaukee Journal*, October 25, 1953.

Mann, Jack. "Danger with a Double A." *Sports Illustrated*, August 1, 1966.

Markus, Robert. "Aaron Now Walks in Brilliant Sun, but . . ." *Chicago Tribune*, September 1, 1969.

Minshaw, Wayne. "Hank's 3000-Hit Dream Born in '54." *Sporting News*, May 23, 1970.

Murray, Jim. "Move Over, Babe . . . Aaron's Playing Right." *Los Angeles Times*, October 1969.

Musick, Phil. "No. 1 in Atlanta." *Pittsburgh Press*, June 9, 1969.

Poinsett, Alex. "The Hank Aaron Nobody Knows." *Ebony*, July 1974.

Rhoden, William. "It Is Time We Took Aaron Into Hearts." *New York Times*, April 9, 1995.

Richman, Milton. "The Trials of Henry Aaron: 'Everyday, It's the Same.'" *Atlanta Constitution*, July 11, 1973.

Smith, Wendell. "End Spring Degradation, Negro Players Ask." *Chicago American*, July 30, 1961.

————. "Integrates Motel-Periled." *Chicago American*, April 5, 1961.

————. "Negro Ballplayers Want Rights in South." *Chicago American*, January 23, 1961.

————. "Negro Players Gain in Equality Bid." *Chicago American*, February 6, 1961.

————. "What a Negro Ballplayer Faces Today in Training." *Chicago American*, April 3, 1961.

Spander, Art. "Home Run King Aaron Not Bitter, Just Honest." *San Francisco Examiner,* June 10, 1993.

Stein, Harry. "Henry Aaron's Golden Autumn." *Sport,* March 1973.

Stump, Al. "Hank Aaron: Public Image vs. Private Reality." *Sport*, August 1964.

Sykes, Tanisha. "Power Hitter Baseball Legend Hank Aaron Scores Big with His Import Dealerships." *Black Enterprise*, June 2004.

Thisted, Red. "Rookie Aaron, 20, Makes Trial Run in Bobby's Shoes." *Milwaukee Journal*, March 24, 1954.

Walker, Don. "Hammerin' Away, Aaron Takes Swing at Players' Union in Drug Fiasco." *Milwaukee Journal Sentinel*, March 5, 2004.

PUBLIC PAPERS

Aaron, Hank. National Baseball Hall of Fame Induction Speech. August 1, 1982, Cooperstown, NY.

Chandler, Albert B. "Happy." National Baseball Hall of Fame Induction Speech. August 1, 1982, Cooperstown, NY.

The Congressional Record. April 9, 1974 and June 13, 1974.

Robinson, Frank. National Baseball Hall of Fame Induction Speech. August 1, 1982, Cooperstown, NY.

Smith, Wendell. Wendell Smith Papers c. 1943–1961, courtesy of the National Baseball Hall of Fame Library, MSB 1.

FILMS, MUSIC, AND WEB SITES

Bauman, Mike. "Bonds Able, But Aaron a Fitting King." Major League Baseball Web site: www.mlb.com. September 4, 2003.

Burns, Ken. *Baseball.* Washington DC: WETA-TV, Florentine Films, 1994.

Henry Aaron: The Life of a Legend. Revere, MA: Fleetwood Recording Co., Inc. 1974.

Tollin, Mike, and Hank Aaron. *Chasing the Dream.* Atlanta: TBS Productions, 1995.

INDEX

About the Author

CHARLIE VASCELLARO is a freelance journalist and regular contributor to Baltimore and Washington, D.C. newspapers and magazines, writing frequently on baseball and travel. A former 20-year resident of Arizona, his work appears annually in Cactus League spring training publications and in Arizona business and travel periodicals. *Hank Aaron* is his second book; Vascellaro has also written a young reader biography of Dominican-born baseball player Manny Ramirez.

Edwards Brothers Malloy
Thorofare, NJ USA
December 18, 2014